This book belongs to

_____

...a woman after God's own heart.

Walking in God's Promises

Elizabeth George

HARVEST HOUSE PUBLISHERS
EUGENE, OREGON

Cover by Terry Dugan Design, Minneapolis, Minnesota

Acknowledgments

As always, thank you to my dear husband, Jim George, M.Div., Th.M., for your able assistance, guidance, suggestions, and loving encouragement on this project.

WALKING IN GOD'S PROMISES
Copyright © 2001 Elizabeth George
Published by Harvest House Publishers
Eugene, Oregon 97402

ISBN 978-0-7369-0301-1 (pbk.)
ISBN 978-0-7369-3343-8 (eBook)

Printed in the United States of America.

15 16 17 18 19 / BP-CF / 15 14 13 12 11 10

Contents

Foreword

For some time I have been looking for Bible studies that I could use each day that would increase my knowledge of God's Word. In my search, I found myself struggling between two extremes: Bible studies that required little time but also had little substance, or studies that were in-depth and demanded more time than I could give. I discovered that I wasn't alone—there were many other women like me who were busy yet desired to spend quality time studying God's Word.

That's why I became excited when Elizabeth George shared her desire to create a series of women's Bible studies that offered in-depth lessons that could be completed in just 15-20 minutes per day. When she completed the first study—on Philippians—I was eager to try it out. I had already studied Philippians many times, but this was the first time I had come to understand exactly how the whole book fit together and how it can truly be lived out in my life. Each lesson was simple but insightful—and was written especially to apply to me as a woman!

In the Woman After God's Own Heart® Bible study series, Elizabeth takes you step by step through the Scriptures, sharing wisdom she has gleaned from more than 20 years as a women's Bible teacher. The lessons are rich and meaningful because they're rooted in God's Word and have been lived out in Elizabeth's life. Her thoughtful and personable guidance makes you feel as though you are studying right alongside her—as if she is personally mentoring you in the greatest aspiration you could ever pursue: to become a woman after God's own heart.

If you're looking for Bible studies that can help you grow stronger in your knowledge of God's Word even in the most demanding of schedules, I know you'll find this series to be a welcome companion in your daily walk with God.

—LaRae Weikert
Vice President, Editorial,
Harvest House Publishers

Before You Begin

In my book *A Woman After God's Own Heart*®, I describe such a woman as one who ensures that God is first in her heart and the Ultimate Priority of her life. Then I share that one crucial way this desire can become reality is by nurturing a heart that abides in God's Word. To do so means that you and I must develop a root system anchored deep in God's Word.

Before you launch into this Bible study, take a moment to think about these aspects of a root system produced by the regular, faithful study of God's Word:

- *Roots are unseen*—You'll want to set aside time in solitude— "underground" if you will—to immerse yourself in God's Word and grow in Him.

- *Roots are for taking in*—Alone and with your Bible in hand, you'll want to take in and feed upon the truths of the Word of God and ensure your spiritual growth.

- *Roots are for storage*—As you form the habit of looking into God's Word, you'll find a vast, deep reservoir of divine hope and strength forming for the rough times.

- *Roots are for support*—Do you want to stand strong in the Lord? To stand firm against the pressures of life? The routine care of your roots through exposure to God's Word will cultivate you into a remarkable woman of endurance.[1]

I'm glad you've chosen this study out of my Woman After God's Own Heart® Bible study series. My prayer for you is that the truths you find in God's Word through this study will further transform your life into the image of His dear Son and empower you to be the woman you seek to be: a woman after God's own heart.

In His love,

Elizabeth George

Beginning the Journey

On a recent drop-in visit to see my almost-two-years-old granddaughter, little Taylor ran to her book corner and brought me her new favorite Golden Book, *The Princess and the Pea*. As she snuggled on my lap and turned the pages, all that she pointed to and commented on could be encompassed in one new word (for her)—*princess*.

That focus, dear one, could describe our study about Sarah—a look at the life of a princess and how she walked (and sometimes didn't walk!) in God's promises. As you and I venture forth together through time and through 13-plus chapters of the Bible with Sarah, you'll no doubt notice two things.

—Two names, Sarai and Sarah. I'll refer to our princess as Sarah throughout.

—Two names, Abram and Abraham. I'll refer to Sarah's husband as Abraham throughout.

Let's pray now before we proceed that we'll both be blessed by the *person* of Sarah and by her walk with God based on faith in His *promises*. As a woman after God's own heart, we have much to learn from this giant of the faith (Hebrews 11:11). For, indeed, we are her "daughters" if we follow in her footsteps of faith and walk in God's promises (1 Peter 3:6).

Now, let the journey begin!

Meeting Sarah

I love it when someone asks me a question of substance, a question that indicates thought on the part of the asker, and that provokes reflection on my part to answer it.

Well, I was recently asked such a question—"Who are your favorite authors, and what kind of books do you read?" Answering the first part of this woman's inquiry was easy. But afterwards I gave great thought to the second part of her question, the part regarding the kind of books I read. In the end I concluded that I read a *lot* of commentaries on the books of the Bible, a *lot* of books on the men and women of the Bible, and a *lot* of biographies of the people of great faith down through the centuries.

All of this to say, I've read a *lot* about the Old Testament princess, Sarah, and her husband, Abraham, the father of our faith.

But right now I want to focus on *you*—what do you know, or what have you heard about Sarah? Here are a few things historians and scholars have to say about her:

- She was a woman of unusual beauty.

  An ancient Jewish commentary on Genesis that was found among the Dead Sea Scrolls said of Sarah's beauty:

  > Of all the virgins and brides
  > That walk beneath the canopy,
  > None can compare with Sarah.[2]

- She was the long-time wife of the patriarch Abraham.

- She was a "chieftainess," a complement to her husband the "chieftain."

- She was the "mother" of a nation and an ancestor of Jesus.

- She is the first woman listed in God's Hall of Faith in Hebrews 11.

- She is the only woman whose age is given in the Old Testament.

- She "is listed as one of the 22 bibical (OT) women worthy of the title 'virtuous woman.'"[3]

- She is described by one scholarly source in this way:

  > What kind of woman was she? Above all, she was the wife of a pioneer. She left the ease of the city for the dangers of a semi-nomadic existence; she left her family to become, with her husband, a stranger in a strange land. She was a beautiful woman; jealous of her husband's love and zealous for her own position; she was a mother who, craving the best for her child, was cruel for his sake. Despite this, later generations considered her a paragon of beauty and piety.... Her

name means princess, and, though the information about her is scanty, we may conclude that the name properly describes the helpmate of the great Patriarch.[4]

This is all exciting information. But the most important words you and I will ever read about Sarah are found in God's Word, the Bible. Indeed, what God Himself has to say about Sarah is paramount. So, dear woman after God's own heart, let's look to the Bible right now for God's input about Sarah, a woman who walked in His promises.

God's Input...

1. The details of Sarah's life begin in Genesis 11:29. Read Genesis 11:27-32 now and note what you learn about Sarah and about the people with whom she was associated.

Terah–

Abram–

Nahor–

Haran–

Lot–

Sarai (Sarah)–

Milcah–

2. What else do you learn from Genesis 20:12?

And from Joshua 24:2?

It is interesting to note that the names of Terah, Laban, Sarah, and Milcah point towards the "moon-god." Also, Ur and Haran were centers of moon worship.[5]

...and Your Heart's Answer

- According to Acts 7:2-4, what launched Sarah's life of faith?

- What does the Bible say about a wife's relationship with her husband in...

Ephesians 5:22–

Colossians 3:18–

Titus 2:5–

- What does the Bible tell us specifically about Sarah as a wife in 1 Peter 3:6?

- And what does the Bible have to say about husbands in...

Genesis 2:24–

Ephesians 5:23 and 25–

Colossians 3:19–

1 Peter 3:7–

- How do you see Sarah and Abraham living out God's pattern for marriage so far?

From the Heart

Up to this point (Genesis 11:27-32), we haven't read of any promises from God given to this choice couple, Sarah and Abraham. However, as we learned from Acts 7:2-4, Abraham had already heard the call of God and was heeding it. And it looks like, according to 1 Peter 3:6, that our Sarah has readily gone about the business of following her Abraham...in faith...and without fear!

Following a husband is, as a book title describes it, "the adventure of being a wife"! And I'm so blessed to be able to think of two examples of such faithful following right away.

First is my pastor's mother. Her husband was a pastor who moved frequently, and it was said of her that whenever her husband phoned home to announce that they were moving (again!), she had the boxes out and the pictures off the wall before he got home from work that day!

Second is my daughter Courtney. Married to a career Navy man, Courtney is ever on the move. With each and every change of assignment, my daughter is cheerfully cleaning out drawers, cupboards, and closets, stopping her newspaper and magazine subscriptions, and purchasing maps of the area where their new home will be.

Neither of these women has allowed her "nesting instinct" to hinder her from walking away from comfort and security...to something greater, to a life of faith. They follow their husbands by faith. And, I'll add, they must trust in the Lord in order to do so.

And so must you, if you want to live a life of faith and walk in God's promises.

Now, before you come to any hasty conclusions, let me quickly say—this is *not* a study about marriage! However you and I will have the opportunity to watch up-close the relationship that Sarah and Abraham enjoyed as a married couple.

Following in faith won't always involve a husband, but for a woman after God's own heart, following God is all about following *someone else!* Be it a parent, a pastor, a boss or supervisor, or a husband, we spend our life following! In Sarah's case, she followed her husband *by faith* as he followed God *by faith*.

May you and I ever follow in Sarah's footsteps in this important area of following!

*L*esson 2

Growing Faith Through Sorrow

Genesis 11:27-32

*P*erhaps one seed of great faith is *lack*. By that I mean that faith many times grows great to fill a void, to fill a lack in some area of our life, to fill in a missing component.

Let's "rewind" for a moment, if you will, and look more closely at a few words in the Bible text from Lesson 1 that inform us of a lack in dear Sarah's life. They are only eight words out of Genesis 11:30 (at least in my Bible), but these eight words speak loudly of pain and suffering, of failure and persecution.

As I think of the many women of great faith I know, I can almost—to a woman—point to some sorrow or tragedy that has served as a seed for growing greater faith. The roll call of those I know includes:

- many widows whose lives now include no husband;

- a writer who writes from her sickbed due to an affliction that will never improve;

- a mother of a dozen children who has lost half of them to death;

- a number of women who have suffered from cancer and live under its ever-present shadow;

- a handful of missionary wives who are married to men who literally "sold all" to follow Christ without the hindrance of home or possessions.

Is there a "lack" in your life, dear one? Is there some sorrow or some missing element? It would be good for you to identify it and keep it in the forefront of your mind as we walk alongside Sarah, whose sorrow was barrenness.

Sarah's faith was forced to grow in the light of God's plan for her life, a plan which included childlessness. I know what my lack is—and has been. But I also give praise to God for His unfailing lovingkindness, His eternal wisdom, and His all-sufficient grace as the "lack" has led to far greater faith in my life!

God's Input...

1. Read again Genesis 11:27-32. Then copy here the eight words from verse 30 that speak of Sarah's sorrow, of Sarah's lack.

2. Sarah was not alone in her difficulty. Note here the path of other great women of faith. Write out the name of each and what the Bible says about her.

Genesis 25:21–

Genesis 29:31; 30:1-2–

Judges 13:2–

1 Samuel 1:2,5-6–

2 Kings 4:12-14–

Luke 1:7–

Barrenness was a stigma and carried a reproach in a culture where blessings were tied to birthright. The previously-barren Elizabeth remarked on this fact when she became pregnant and uttered that God "looked on me to take away my reproach among men" (Luke 1:25).

...and Your Heart's Answer

- We've already "rewound" in our study. Now I want us to "fast forward" in the life of Sarah. We'll look at each of these passages more in-depth in the days to come, but in this lesson I want you to note God's many promises to Abraham and Sarah.

Genesis 12:2–

Genesis 12:7–

Genesis 13:15–

Genesis 15:4–

Genesis 17:19–

Genesis 18:10–

- If and when the barren, childless Sarah were tempted to give up on God and His promise for a family, as a woman of faith (Hebrews 11:11) she could cling to the promise of God to give Abraham a son.

  Here's a little grid to help you, too, to turn your heart to God's promises when you are tempted to dwell on your own lack: How do God's promises strengthen our faith?

> –They *provide* confidence for the future.
>
> –They *prove* God's faithfulness.
>
> –They *preview* God's plan.
>
> –They *produce* contentment.[6]

- And now, dear daughter of Sarah, what has God promised to *you* that *you* cling to regularly? What promises from God guide you like beacons through dark times? When there seems to be no hope, what promise or promises from God serve as a rising sun—or at least a rising star— directing your faith back to faith's Source? Stop now and give God glory as you acknowledge the power of His promises to assist you in your walk through life.

From the Heart

We'll soon see more—lots more!—of Sarah's walk and her growing faith in God's promises (and even a little bit of her lack of faith at times). But for now I want you to go back to the *lack* you thought of and named earlier in this lesson. Keeping your answer in mind, look up these marvelous promises from God and jot down the heart of each promise and a few thoughts on how you can put them to use in your situation.

God's promise   *Your application*

• Psalm 23:1

• Psalm 34:8-10

• Psalm 84:11

• Ecclesiastes 3:11

• Philippians 4:13

• 1 Corinthians 10:13

Lesson 3

Leaving Home

Genesis 11:27-32

*I*well remember my husband Jim's phone call to me early (5:30 A.M.!) one morning many years ago—a phone call that altered the life of each person in our family. Jim was on a missions excursion through Asia. More specifically, he was in a phone booth in the Singapore airport. In 11 words, our lives changed, for Jim asked, "Hey, how would you like to move to Singapore and minister?"

I'm not sure how or why, but (perhaps because I was missing Jim so much...or because it was so early that I wasn't thinking too clearly) I blurted out, "Sure! Where is it?"

And off we went to be missionaries in Singapore!

Our lesson today takes a closer look at Sarah's "call," if you will. No, it wasn't a phone call, but it was nevertheless a "call" from God to her husband Abraham, a call to leave their home in Ur of the Chaldees and trek to Canaan. Let's see how Sarah handled leaving home.

God's Input...

1. Reread Genesis 11:27-32. We've already noted the names of Sarah and Abraham's family members. And we've already registered the fact of Sarah's childlessness. Now I want you to pinpoint the following places on the map provided on page 153 of this book:

Ur of the Chaldees

Haran

Canaan

2. How far did Sarah and Abraham's traveling party make it on the road to Canaan (verse 31)?

What happened in Haran, causing them to stop there (verses 31-32)?

Note that scholars calculate that, after leaving Ur, Abraham resided in Haran approximately another 15 years before finally journeying on with his relatives into the land of Canaan.[7]

We also know that Haran was a city just as idolatrous as Ur, and was still in the land of Mesopotamia. And here God's people of faith settled for 15 years.

...and Your Heart's Answer

As Sarah "walked" with Abraham as he followed God, her path led her out of Ur of the Chaldees. Scholars tell us that Ur was a bustling commercial center. Located in the region of Mesopotamia on the Persian Gulf and bordered by the Euphrates River, Ur was one of the leading cities in the world. The people there were intelligent and educated. And yet God was clearly leading Sarah and Abraham out of the idolatrous Ur of the Chaldees and away from their home-land—the known land—and into the unknown land.

• What does Psalm 37:23-24 tell us about those who walk in the path and pattern of God's will?

God generally reveals His will in stages. So, my dear new traveling friend, wherever you are, don't settle in too quickly. And don't sink your roots down too far. For, as George Müller wrote of Psalm 37:23-24,

The steps—*and stops*—of the godly are ordered by the Lord.

And He delights in his way [and] upholds him with His hand.[8]

• Still yet we haven't read of any promises from God to Sarah and Abraham. However, what do you learn about Sarah and Abraham's faith in Hebrews 11:8?

- God doesn't say whether Sarah and Abraham were obedient or disobedient to move out only half-way to the promised land and then settle for a while. But God does say that this faithful twosome *did* leave home in order to follow after Him. Can you think of a time when God clearly asked you to leave home, or your nest, or your comfort zone, and follow Him? Share it here, please.

Or can you think of a "call" God has issued to you to leave something or someone so that you can better follow Him? And you are refusing to do so or delaying your obedience? Share it here now, and then enjoy a sobering thought from writer and lecturer Elisabeth Elliot:

*D*elayed obedience is disobedience.

- Now look at these few specifics that are clear callings to you and me as women after God's own heart to leave something or someone and follow after God. Jot down the gist of each calling.

1 John 2:15-17–

Colossians 3:1-2–

2 Corinthians 6:14-18–

From the Heart

Home is where the heart is. I know that you as a woman have probably heard this sentimental saying.

But it's true! As you, a woman after God's own heart, set about to follow Him with your whole heart, then, wherever you are will be home, because you'll be in the center of His will!

Dear friend, I've just returned from South Africa where I traveled with my husband Jim to visit our church's missionaries. These families are all friends of ours, and the men are former students whom Jim taught at The Master's Seminary. What did I see there on the mission field? And what did I witness in these missionary wives?

I saw women who had given up family and friends and homes and possessions to follow their husbands to this far-away country to serve God. I saw women who live in unsafe places and pray each and every day for literal physical safety for their families. I saw women who never go out in their cars after dark because to do so is to put their lives at risk. I saw women sleeping on the floor so Jim and I could sleep in their beds.

On and on the list of these women's sacrifices goes. And why is the list so long? Because they have given up all to follow their husbands...who are following God.

But are you surprised to hear me report that each and every one of these modern-day Sarahs is at "home"? At home in her setting? At home in a foreign country? At home in her heart?

No, joy is theirs *in* their situation because, you see, they are women after God's own heart, women who walk in God's precious promises...wherever He leads them. He never changes, and neither do His promises.

I'm praying that you, too, dear one, may be at home... wherever God leads you!

Walking and Worshiping

Genesis 12:1-9

*D*o you have a favorite hymn, my friend? There's no doubt that one of my favorite old-time hymns is "He Leadeth Me." I often find myself humming its chorus,

> He leadeth me, He leadeth me,
> By His own hand He leadeth me;
> His faithful foll'wer I would be,
> For by His hand He leadeth me.

Most hymns come to us out of tragedy. But not this one. It was born out of preacher Joseph H. Gilmore's sense of blessedness and awe at the fact that Almighty God Himself leads us! Evidently Christians for almost a century have been equally moved by the simple fact of God's leading, because this hymn, possibly more than any other, has been translated into other languages.

Today we get to journey alongside Sarah and Abraham as God, too, was leading them. So hum a few bars...and let's get going!

God's Input...

1. Read again Acts 7:2-4 and note the stages of Sarah and Abraham's path as they migrated to Canaan:

   Stage 1: verses 2 and 3–

   Stage 2: verse 4a–

   Stage 3: verse 4b–

2. As we learned in our previous lesson, Sarah and Abraham stayed in Haran approximately 15 years. Now, as you read Genesis 12:1-3, note the content of God's encounter with Abraham:

   Abraham's part—verse 1–

   God's part—shown to us in six promises. (Four promises are in verse 2 and two promises are in verse 3). List them here.

   Promise #1–

Promise #2–

Promise #3–

Promise #4–

Promise #5–

Promise #6–

3. Now read Genesis 12:4-6 and chart where Sarah and Abraham's path took them on the map on page 153 as they—by faith—left the known for the unknown.

Who made up this little band of faithful followers?

What was Abraham's age?

And remember, Sarah was ten years younger than Abraham. So, what then was Sarah's age as they moved out toward the promised land?

4. Finally, read Genesis 12:7-9. What promise did God make in verse 7?

And what was Abraham's response in verse 7?

Chart on the map Sarah and Abraham's next movement along their path of faithfully following God (verse 8).

What act of worship was repeated?

And where did Abraham next move his cargo and kinfolk (verse 9)? (Don't forget your map on page 153!)

...and Your Heart's Answer

As we inspect the pattern of Sarah's walk with Abraham and with God, note that when Sarah and Abraham left Haran...

✔ They took their nephew Lot with them. Family was taken along and taken care of in the absence of the family patriarch, Abraham's father.

✔ They took all of their possessions with them. They left nothing behind to return to or to pull on their hearts!

✔ They took all their people with them. Their servants went along with them as they followed God.

✔ They encountered the Canaanites, descendants of Canaan, the grandson of Noah (Genesis 9:22). They inhabited most of what would later be called Palestine and practiced an immoral pagan religion.

Sarah's walk—As you consider the pattern of Sarah's walk, think about your own walk with God. Put yourself in Sarah's place. Would you have been able to leave home and family and friends to follow God and your husband? Why or why not?

My husband told me of a woman who lives on a lake in middle America and thoroughly enjoys the quiet setting and leisurely pace. Her husband had a career opportunity that would bring him to Los Angeles, but she had no desire to relocate, expecially to Los Angeles. Leaving her lake to follow her husband would mean taking a risk, making a move, and growing her faith through those changes. In this woman's case, her comfort seemed to be causing her faith to stop growing.

Are there areas in your life where you need to be more like Sarah and "get out" or "leave" something or someone you are clinging to? Explain your answer, please.

Sarah's worship–So far we've seen Abraham and his clan stop to erect altars and worship God two times—in Genesis 12:7 and 8. Well, my friend, get used to this scene! We'll witness it many more times in our travels with Sarah and Abraham! These followers of God were also worshipers of God. They delighted in declaring their utter dependence upon God and their wholehearted dedication to Him. Each altar built was yet another proclamation of their devotion to Jehovah and their belief in His promises to them. They made a clean break from the pagan religions of their ancestors.

Take a minute and look at the life and walk of Rachel in Genesis 31:17-30. How did her walk with God differ from Sarah's?

Now, how about you? Are there any old ways or old things that you may be failing to cast aside? Any "idols" you may still be carrying along as you seek to walk with God? Are you following in the pattern of Sarah's walk of faith or in Rachel's lack of faith? Be specific.

From the Heart

Walking and *worshiping. Walking* and *worshiping.* These words most definitely describe Sarah and Abraham's journey to Canaan and their acknowledgment of God's leading!

Why not stop right this minute in your *walk* and *worship* the Lord? Or, as one has expressed it of Abraham, he "kept up his correspondence with heaven."[9] Sarah and Abraham paused in their progression to give thanks and pay reverence to God for His protection and His promises. Each pause was proof that God was at the center of their hearts and lives. The act of worship never fails to remind us...

...of our dependence upon God
...of our need to call upon His name
...of our thankfulness to God for His many kindnesses
...of His desire for our obedience

Taking a Side Trip to Egypt

Genesis 12:10-20

*H*ow do *you* make decisions? Have you ever given this question much thought? Perhaps you will after today's lesson, because in it we get a good look at a decision Abraham made—a bad decision made out of cowardice—that created a frightening situation for our beautiful Sarah. Let's find out about a little side trip to Egypt Abraham and his company of family, servants, and animals took.

God's Input...

1. Read Genesis 12:10-20. What new condition arose in Sarah and Abraham's life (verse 10)?

And how is this condition described?

And what did Abraham decide to do?

2. As Sarah and Abraham neared Egypt, what did Abraham fear (verses 11-12)?

What plan did he propose as a solution (verse 13)?

3. Sure enough, what happened (verse 14)?

And what happened to Sarah (verse 15)?

And how was Abraham treated because of Sarah (verse 16)?

4. How did God come to Sarah's rescue (verse 17)?

Now how was Abraham treated (verses 18-19)?

In the end (verse 20), Pharaoh in essence said, "Take her and be gone!" and sent God's chosen couple out of the country under armed escort. A pagan and a heathen was used to *rebuke* and to *re-route* Abraham and to get him back on track.

...and Your Heart's Answer

Indeed, situations like Sarah entered into are never pleasant or simple! But this much we do know:

- We know the role of a wife (please review these scriptures)–

  Ephesians 5:22–

  Colossians 3:18–

  Titus 2:5–

  1 Peter 3:1-2–

- We also know how highly exalted Sarah is for her faith:

  Hebrews 11:11–How was Sarah's faith exhibited here?

  1 Peter 3:5-6–What words stand out most to you?

Sarah seems to have said nothing during this ordeal. She seems to have submitted to Abraham's request that she pose as his sister (which was half-a-truth and half-a-lie!). Her trust in her husband and in God may have been so complete as to overrule any fears or thoughts of the consequences of her husband's actions. Question: How are you at trusting God, even in the midst of difficult situations?

Perhaps some of these promises will help you in your walk with God as you, too, perhaps are led on a few "side trips to Egypt." Hide these promises in your heart and take them with you. Note the promise of each:

Psalm 34:15–

Lamentations 3:22-24–

Matthew 6:26–

(And, as the comforting Christian hymn reminds us, "His eye is on the sparrow, and I know He watches me."[10])

1 Peter 3:12–

From the Heart

Sarah and Abraham's dilemma brings up a good question for you and me as we seek to be women after God's own heart—How can we know God's will? How can we make right decisions—God's decisions? We couldn't help but notice that Abraham did not appear to consult with God regarding the path he and Sarah should take. He did what we so often do—act first and pray later!

If nothing else, dear reader, I hope and pray that this scene from the life of Sarah makes you want to be more careful regarding the important area of decision-making. I know it affected me in this way! So here's a helpful "recipe," if you will, for decision-making and the will of God, for determining the will of God.[11]

Word of God—Always consult God's Word. Our first thought should be, "What does God's Word say about a situation or a choice like this?" Does the decision you are about to make violate any teaching from God's Word? Be sure you are like the Bereans who searched the Scriptures daily to find out the truth (Acts 17:11). As one of my favorite truths about

God's Word declares, "The counsel of the LORD stands forever, the plans of His heart to all generations" (Psalm 33:11).

Wise counsel—Look to others in the body of Christ. Seek out those who are gifted and known for their biblical wisdom and discernment (1 Corinthians 12:8). What does your husband say? Your pastor (Hebrews 13:7)? An older woman (Titus 2:3)?

Weigh the consequences—Ask questions like these: What is the worst thing that could happen? Would anyone be hurt? What would a good decision be? Is there a better choice I could make? And what would the best decision be?

Wait on the Lord in prayer—Have you prayed about your situation and your decision? How much? Do you need to fast as you wait for God's leading? Praying is one way we consult the Lord. And don't rush! Very few situations call for an on-the-spot decision. And even when one does, you can still shoot up an "arrow prayer" to God as Nehemiah did between breaths as he answered the king in Nehemiah 2:4-5.

Purpose now, dear follower of Sarah, to join the order of those wise and careful Christians who consult God's Word and wise counselors, and who carefully weigh consequences and wait on the Lord in prayer. This recipe could perhaps help *you* to avoid a few "side trips to Egypt" yourself! As British preacher F. B. Meyer passes on to us, "If you are willing to know, [God] will make you know somehow. If not one way, then another."[12]

Lesson 6

Moving Back to Canaan

Genesis 13:1-12

Moving. Just say this word and most women cringe as nightmarish memories resurface. At one time, I read a list of the most stress-causing events in life and discovered that #1 is the death of a spouse, followed by #2, moving!

Well, our sister Sarah is on the move again in this lesson. So far in our five lessons she's moved...

from Ur	☛	to Haran (Genesis 11:31)
from Haran	☛	to Shechem in Canaan (Genesis 12:6)
from Shechem	☛	to Bethel (Genesis 12:8)
from Bethel	☛	to Egypt (Genesis 12:10)

And today we witness her moving...

from Egypt   ☞   to Bethel (Genesis 13:3)
from Bethel   ☞   to Hebron (Genesis 13:18)

Let's see what happened on this latest move and learn more from Sarah and Abraham about walking in God's promises. (Remember your map on page 153!)

God's Input...

1. As you remember, the pharaoh of Egypt had severely reprimanded Abraham for lying regarding Sarah, for saying she was his sister instead of his wife—a half-truth which was also a half-lie! In what direction did Abraham's party move (verse 1)? (Don't forget to chart this move on the map in the back of this book.)

   And who went along with Sarah and Abraham (verse 1)?

   How is Abraham described in verse 2?

   And how is Lot described in verse 5?

2. What did Abraham do when he returned to Bethel (verse 4)?

   And what did Lot's company do when they returned to Bethel, and why (verses 6-7)?

How did Abraham resolve this problem (verses 8-9)?

3. As I studied Lot's decision-making process, it seemed to fall into the following progression. Read verses 10-13 and see if you agree that his actions might well be named "Four Steps Toward Disaster." There's no doubt that Lot's choices revealed his character!

Lot looked.   What did he see (verse 10)?

Lot lusted.   What did he want (verse 10)?

Lot landed.   What did he choose (verse 11)?

Lot left.   Where did he go (verses 11-13)?
                   (Again, use your map.)

For your information...travellers say that, from the vantage point where Lot and Abraham most likely stood, one can see the Jordan River and the broad meadows on either bank, and the waving line of greenery which marks the course of the stream.[13]

4. After Lot left Abraham's company, the Lord appeared again to Abraham in the land of Canaan with two promises. What was Promise #1 (verse 15)?

How vast was the land (verse 14)?

What was Promise #2 (verse 16)?

How "vast" would Abraham's descendants prove to be (verse 16)?

What was Abraham's final act in this chapter (verse 18)?

...and Your Heart's Answer

On the move. Back and forth. Lowing cattle and braying bulls. The smell of animals and the scorch of hot sand. Journeying, caravanning...and moving! This seems to have been the emerging pattern of Sarah's walk.

But don't you imagine that the family feud over possessions caused more stress than a lifestyle-on-the-move? However, by all accounts, Sarah's husband Abraham handled the tension unselfishly, magnanimously, generously, practically, and wisely. He appears to have been a good-natured man who was disturbed and distressed over a family problem, who took the initiative and willingly forfeited something small (family wealth) to gain something large (family relationships).

These notes give us insight into the wisdom of Abraham's dealings with his family and teach us how to respond in difficult family situations:

Take the initiative to resolve it.

Let others have first choice,

even if it means not getting what you want.

Put family peace above other desires.[14]

- What do these New Testament scriptures teach you and me about handling people problems?

Romans 12:10,18–

Philippians 2:3-4–

- Beloved, are there people problems you are embroiled in at the moment? How do the lives of Sarah and Abraham and their dealings with Lot instruct you? What must you do to walk in the pattern of their noble example?

From the Heart

It occurred to me as I studied this scene that Sarah and Abraham may have been disheartened and sorrowful as they watched Lot leave. He was their beloved relative, their blood-kin. They had traveled nearly two decades together. Surely Lot was like a son to this childless couple!

But God...oh, the goodness of God! In His perfect timing, He spoke once again to Abraham, bearing His gracious gift of a pair of promises to encourage His friend (James 2:23).

Do you ever feel disheartened or sorrowful? Does it ever seem like you are staring into a hopeless future? A frightening future? Take heart, dear woman after God's own heart. You, too, have the exceedingly great and precious promises of God available to your sore heart. Therefore:

- Never underestimate the value of God's promises. Lot may have received the paradise, but Abraham received the promise.

- Never underestimate the power of even one of God's promises to encourage you and give you hope. (And, I might add, never fail to encourage *others* with the promises of God!)

- Never fail to look to the promises of God in your times of need. God said to Abraham, "Lift your eyes now...." The psalmist wrote, "I will lift up my eyes" (Psalm 121:1). God's promises are like shooting stars across the darkest of skies. Don't look down. No, instead, look up! Look up to a "heaven" full of God's sparkling promises.

- Never fail to celebrate each promise from God, and to worship in wonder.

esson 7

Being Courageous

Genesis 14:1-24

owardice and *confidence*. How could two such opposing words describe one man? Well, they do. Both describe Abraham.

We witnessed Abraham's cowardice in his dealings with Pharaoh during a time of famine when he lied about Sarah being his wife. And today we witness his confidence as he swiftly dons battle gear and flies to the rescue of his nephew Lot. God's account of Abraham's courageous assault states that he armed his servants and went out swiftly. As the Hebrew language portrays it, Abraham *drew out* to war quickly (Genesis 14:14), just as a sword is quickly drawn out from its scabbard. Action was sudden and decisive, and with confidence.

God has lessons for us today, dear woman after God's own heart, lessons we can learn about kinfolk and confidence.

God's Input....

Although Sarah was not a direct participant in the following events, we do gain great insight into the path of her life.

1. Read Genesis 14:1-12. In the simplest of words, what happened, according to verses 8 and 9?

   How did the battle turn out (verses 10-11)?

   What else occurred (verse 12)?

2. Now read Genesis 14:13-16. What did Abraham do when he learned the news about his nephew Lot (verse 14)?

   In the simplest of words, what is happening in verses 14-16?

   How did it end (verse 16)?

3. Now read Genesis 14:17-21. What two kings are specifically named who went out to meet Abraham (verses 17 and 18)?

   What did Melchizedek, king of Salem, give to Abraham (verse 18)?

And what did the king of Sodom desire to give to Abraham (verse 21)?

4. Finally, read Genesis 14:22-24. How did Abraham respond to Melchizedek, the king of Salem (verse 20)?

And how did he respond to the king of Sodom (verses 22-24)?

Why (verse 23)?

...and Your Heart's Answer

There's no doubt after reading this chapter that war filled Sarah and Abraham's land. Here we witness groups of kings at war, carrying out slaughtering raids. Soon Sarah's land was surrounded by war and warring armies.

But when Abraham's nephew Lot was taken by such a group of plunderers, that made all the difference in the world! In a flash (just as a sword is swiftly drawn out of its sheath), Sarah's husband Abraham and 318 of their ready-for-war servants swiftly rode out to rescue their family member who was at risk. What was the outcome of Abraham's efforts that took him approximately 120-150 miles (verse 16)? (Don't forget to look at your map on page 153.)

- *Sarah*—As I think about the pattern of Sarah's life, I think of her as probably...

    ...left at home alone,

    ...and for quite a long while (it was a long journey!),

...without her husband and without 318 of the male
  servants who were trained bodyguards.

I hope that Sarah, the great woman of faith, trusted in the
Lord at this time. Nothing is said about her, but I like to
think that she did.

But now for the ultimate question: Does any part of this
description fit any part of your life? Have you ever been
left at home...alone...for quite a long while...without your
husband or any others to protect you? And do you trust
the Lord when you are alone? Share a few details.

This book is about walking in the promises of God. How
does the promise of Psalm 46:1-2 encourage you for such
situations?

- *Lot*—Lot was definitely in the wrong place at the wrong
  time. We'll see more of this later, but how does Galatians
  6:7 apply to Lot at this time?

What are the things you are desiring most? (Or, put
another way, what are you sowing?) And how does Lot's
downfall serve as a warning?

- *Melchizedek*—We don't want to leave this chapter
  without noting the importance of Abraham's encounter
  with Melchizedek, king of Salem. This was no ordinary
  king! Melchizedek's name means "righteous king" and
  Salem was ancient Jerusalem. He had never appeared
  before...and he never appeared again. But he worshiped

and served God Most High (verses 18-19) just as Abraham did. How is he referred to in Hebrews 7:1-2?

• *Abraham*—Here in Genesis 14 we see a few other evidences of Abraham's faith and character. What was his response to the news of his family member Lot's demise?

How did he treat Melchizedek, king of Salem?

How did he treat the king of Sodom?

Based on what you know about Melchizedek thus far, how would you explain the difference between Abraham's two responses to these two kings?

From the Heart

We began this study with two opposing words—*cowardice* and *confidence*. And now I want us to turn our hearts to answering the question, Where does courage come from?

As we consider Abraham's heart toward God and his actions in these verses, his confidence appears to have come from:

—Being in the center of God's will and doing the right thing—*Abraham* was in the right place at the right time! And Abraham had no desire to war against kings or to gain wealth—only to rescue his family member.

— Being prepared—Abraham was a man of peace, yet disciplined for war. He had diligently and wisely trained his servants for battle. "We never know when we will be called upon to complete difficult tasks. Like Abram, we should prepare for those times and then take courage from God when they come."[15]

— Being bold—"Those that venture in a good cause, with a good heart, are under the special protection of a good God, and have reason to hope for a good issue."[16]

— Being assisted by God's grace—Lot's prize was so quickly lost, but Abraham's small resources were so effective—318 men against an army! God Most High delivered his enemies into his hand (verse 20).

*L*esson 8

Trusting the Lord

Genesis 15:1-11

*W*hat is true faith? The book of Hebrews says that faith is "the substance of things *hoped for,* the evidence of things *not seen*" (Hebrews 11:1, emphases added). As this verse points out, true faith does not need visible proof.

Another fact about faith is that it is only as valid as its object. For instance, all of us have faith in something—family, job, country, etc. But true saving faith is putting our trust in the God of Genesis 15. In this lesson we'll see Abraham do just that. We'll witness his believing God for things *not seen*. And, dear one, it was *that* faith that saved him (and, as we'll soon see, it is that same faith that saves you and me)!

God's Input....

1. As we step into another section of the life story of Sarah and Abraham, you'll notice again that Sarah is not mentioned. But, like any wife, Sarah was affected by all that went on in her husband's life, especially his meetings with God. Take a minute to look at these meetings again and note the gist of each encounter.

   Genesis 12:1-3–

   Genesis 12:7–

   Genesis 13:14-17–

2. Now read Genesis 15:1-6. The Bible text begins, "After these things...." Quickly recount the highlights of chapter 14 to clarify *what* things.

   What were God's first words to Abraham in Genesis 15:1?

   And how does God describe Himself to Abraham (verse 1)?

   To further clarify, here God promises to be Abraham's "shield" against foreign warriors. God's words were calculated to give the fearful Abraham hope, courage, and faith.

3. Perhaps Abraham was concerned about the danger to his family from possible retaliation from the kings he had just defeated. Or about the potentiality of poverty, as he had just rejected the generous offer of goods from the king of Sodom *and* was forced to live on and by the left-overs of Lot's choice of the fertile lands. We don't know for sure. But what does verse 2 reveal that was definitely on Abraham's mind?

What conclusion and solution had Abraham come up with (verses 2-3)?

And what did God *say* to put His friend Abraham's heart to rest (verse 4)?

And what did God *do* to put His friend Abraham's heart to rest (verse 5)?

4. Write out the oft-quoted verse 6 here. Then check off each reference below as you look it up in your Bible:

___ Romans 4:3

___ Galatians 3:6

___ James 2:23

5. Finish this section by reading Genesis 15:7-11. After God reassured Abraham of an heir, Abraham asked for some kind of visible sign. What did Abraham ask God in verse 8?

And briefly, how did God answer (verses 9-10)?

Dr. Gene Getz explains what's happening here in this way: "God answered by use of a common ceremony, one that was familiar to Abraham. In those days two parties would enter into a covenant by selecting certain animals and birds, cutting them in half...and laying them out in two lines. Then both parties of the covenant would pass between the lines to confirm the contract. Either party who then violated the contract would be subject to the same fate as the animals–death."[17]

...and Your Heart's Answer

As I contemplated this section of our study, it seems to contain two issues:

• *A Child*—We always think of a couple's childlessness as especially sad for the woman. But it obviously bothered Abraham. He thought about it...a lot! And talked with God about it often!

And time was obviously passing. At least three times prior to this encounter in Abraham and Sarah's walk with God, God had promised to make them into a great nation and to give them descendants. And still there was no child! No doubt they wondered and possibly worried and wavered. However...

—Regarding problems—they talked to God often about their desires and problems.

—Regarding promises—God never failed to repeat His promises and to reassure His choice couple with promise upon promise!

Is this true of the pattern of your walk, my friend? Do you take your *problems* to God and talk with Him often regarding them? And do you enjoy the repetition and reassurance of His *promises* to you as revealed in His Word? Take a minute to reflect on your problems and God's promises. Are you trusting the Lord? Please write out an answer and an explanation.

* *A Covenant*—As we read above, this sort of covenant was generally between two people. However, in this case the patriarch Abraham did not pass between the animals. Why? Because in this transaction Abraham was bound by nothing. He had asked for a sign from God, and God was pleased to give him a sign. Also this covenant was to be kept from the Godward side alone. Only the Lord Himself could fulfill its promises, which were unconditional.

From the Heart

So far in the eight lessons of our study we have not yet considered your relationship with God, dear one. And I think this is the right place to do just that. This particular study on "Trusting the Lord" contains one of the key verses in the entire Bible—"And [Abraham] believed in the LORD, and He accounted it to him for righteousness" (Genesis 15:6).

So, because faith is only as valid as its object, let's see what the object of your faith is and should be. Answer these questions yes or no and explain your answer.

Do you believe the truth of Romans 3:23?–

Do you believe the truth of Romans 6:23?–

Do you believe in the truth of Romans 5:8?–

Do you believe and confess the truths of Romans 10:9?–

Are you God's child, my friend? Have you *believed* unto righteousness? Are you trusting in Jesus Christ for His promise of life everlasting (John 10:28)? Please explain. If your answers here are *yes*, then you, dear friend, are truly a woman after God's own heart, one who is truly trusting in the Lord!

Lesson 9

Looking to the Future
Genesis 15:12-21

As I mentioned in our previous lesson, Genesis 15:6, which describes Abraham's faith, is one of the key verses (and truths) in the Bible. Before we move ahead and "look to the future," I want us to take a minute or two and look back at that verse,

And he believed in the LORD, and
He accounted it to him for righteousness.

When Abraham trusted in God and believed His Word and His promise, God honored his faith: God counted (or reckoned, or considered) it to Abraham for righteousness. In other words, Abraham was justified or counted righteous in the Lord's eyes on the basis of his faith. As Romans 4:20-22 declares of Abraham,

He did not waver at the promise of God through unbelief, but was strengthened in faith, giving glory to God, and being fully convinced that what He had promised He was also able to perform. And therefore "it was accounted to him for righteousness."

God noticed Abraham's faith, and God considered Abraham righteous. Salvation came to Abraham as a result of his *faith* in God and in God's Word, not as a result of any human *works*.

And, dear one, what is true of Abraham's faith and Abraham's salvation is true also of yours. *Your* salvation is due to your *faith* in God—not in any *works*. I like these two thoughts from the *Life Application Bible:*[18]

- Faith is the confidence that God is who He says He is and does what He says He will do.

- It was faith—not perfection—that made Abraham right in God's eyes.

Now, let's turn our focus forward and look to the future!

God's Input....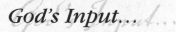

1. Read Genesis 15:12. What is the time of day (verses 12 and 17)?

What happened to Abraham (verses 12 and 18)?

2. Make a list of the facts God gave Abraham...

...regarding Abraham and his future (verse 15)—

...regarding Abraham's future descendants in—

Verse 13—

Verse 14—

Verse 16—

...regarding Abraham's future land (verses 18-21).

...and Your Heart's Answer

- A significant part of Abraham's encounter with God in the dead blackness of night was his vision of God. Read again Genesis 15:17. The sign of the smoking pot or oven and the flaming torch served as a visible assurance that the covenant God was making with Abraham regarding the future of his descendants was real.

  Sarah was not present at this very personal talk Abraham had with God. But what affects a husband usually affects his wife! I've wondered what Sarah thought when (and if) she heard about Abraham's scary evening filled with killing animals, laying them out on the ground, shooing away vultures, sleeping amidst the carcasses, and experiencing a vision of God!

But Abraham's every interaction with God held promise for Sarah, too. Her husband was a godly man—one who regularly talked with God, listened to God, walked with God, and followed God. What does Genesis 19:27 say was apparently one of Abraham's habits?

What was the apparent pattern of Jesus according to Mark 1:35?

And Mark 6:31?

And Luke 6:12?

• Are you married to a Christian mate? If so, how do you respond when your husband wants to spend time with God? To get up early (which usually means going to bed early!) for a quiet time? To attend a men's retreat (which usually means being gone from home!)? To take a Bible class (gone again!)? Be honest. Also jot down any changes you need to make.

Also, how do you and your children benefit from his times with God?

• And perhaps this is a good time to ask, if you are married to a Christian mate who does *not* desire to spend time with God—how do you respond to this situation?

Are you faithful to pray for God to move upon your husband's heart? Are you faithful to pray for God to bring another man along to encourage his spiritual walk? Again, are there any changes you need to make?

- And, if your husband is not a Christian, are you faithful to love, honor, and respect him...without a word (1 Peter 3:1-2)? Are you faithful to pray for God to open your husband's heart to the Savior? Are you living a godly life in front of your husband, so that he is blessed by your consistent example? Once again, what changes should—and *will*—you make?

- Now, if you are single *or* married, answer this: Are *you* following in Abraham's and Jesus' pattern of faithfulness in *your* devotional life, in *your* walk with God? Are *you* getting up early, attending a Bible study, going on retreats, and enrolled in a Bible class, so that *you* benefit from time with God? What changes do you need to make so that you are regularly meeting with the Lord?

From the Heart

Well, my friend, God truly did give Abraham's descendants a great land that stretched from the gates of Egypt to the mighty Euphrates! And God truly did continue to make Abraham's offspring as numerous as the stars!

Yes, God had definitely mapped out Sarah and Abraham's lives and promised them a glorious future—and He's mapped out your future as well. And your path, just like Sarah and Abraham's, is posted with God's promises all along the way. Indeed, God's promises are God's gifts to us, dear one. So as you walk along life's path...

...look for them as you read His Word.

...gather them as you would gather diamonds that were lying at your feet.

...memorize them to draw upon as a resource in times of trouble.

...use them when life's path grows dark and foreboding.

...share them with others who need the light of their assurance.

You need never look to the future without the light of God's promises to illuminate the way!

Lesson 10

Waiting on God

Genesis 16:1-6

Everyone is looking for success. Just visit any bookstore and behold the number of "how-to" books that tout formulas for sure success!

Well, dear friend, you and I know that the Bible is the Ultimate Book on "success." Between its beautiful covers is a vast sea of wisdom and divine laws, of precepts and principles, of teachings and explanations, of instructions on how to do things—all things and anything—God's way.

The Bible is also full of amazing people. There's no doubt that the men and women of the Bible make fascinating character studies. Many of them show us *the right way* to do things. But some show us quite vividly *the wrong way* to do things.

Sadly, in today's lesson, Sarah fits the not-so-flattering category. Let's proceed and see what lessons we can learn from

Sarah about the importance of waiting on God. Sarah, you see, was in a hurry...but God was not. As author Ben Patterson queries in his masterful book titled *Waiting*,

Isn't that the way it so often seems to be with God? You desperately want something that you don't have, something apparently legitimate and worthwhile. And you're forced to wait for it. There's no end in sight, and the pain becomes a dull, daily ache. And you can do nothing without thinking of what you are waiting for. Do you ever think that God is taking his own sweet time with you?[19]

God's Input...

1. What does Genesis 16:1 reveal about the path of Sarah's life?

Remember (once again)...that barrenness was a stigma to a man and woman in Sarah's day (not to mention a tremendous heartache!). To be childless was considered a calamity and a disgrace for any Hebrew wife, and was even suspicioned to be a sign of judgment from God for secret sins.

Just a personal note—I well remember celebrating my fifth anniversary of marriage. Jim and I were having a lovely (and rare!) dinner out. And there I sat, crying and bawling. Why? Because we had no babies yet. The Lord had not chosen to bless us with one of the desires of our hearts.

2. But can you imagine being married some 25-plus years and not having the children you so yearned for? This was the path of Sarah's life, the path God requested that she walk with Him. Look again at these scriptures for a quick review. We've already learned that...

...Sarah had no children and was barren (Genesis 11:30).

...Sarah and Abraham rested in Haran 15 years after God told Abraham to move and promised him descendants (see Lesson 3).

...Sarah and Abraham have now been in Canaan, the promised land, for a good 10 years (Genesis 16:3)...and God has continued to promise Abraham an heir.

3. Now read Genesis 16:1-3. According to verse 1, what is one possession Sarah owned (that she had perhaps acquired in Egypt)?

How did Sarah decide to put Hagar to use (verse 2)?

And what was Abraham's response to Sarah's great idea (verse 2)?

(I personally call these verses "Falling from Faith to Finagling." *Finagling* means to maneuver and manipulate by cleverness and craftiness. How sad to watch and witness Sarah, a woman after God's own heart, a woman known for her faith, failing to wait on God and faltering and stooping to such low means of getting what she wanted. I mean, this is *Sarah*, the woman who has walked in faith alongside her husband looking to God's promise for a son for more than 25 years! Anyway...)

Looking back, how had God revealed Himself to Sarah and Abraham in...

Genesis 14:22?–

Genesis 15:1?–

And yet Sarah could not trust God for one more day! She could not walk in God's promises and wait on Him just one more day!

4. Now read Genesis 16:4-6. What happened next (verse 4)?

How did Hagar respond (verse 4)?

How did Sarah respond to Hagar's response (verse 5)?

And how did Abraham respond to Sarah's response to Hagar's response (verse 6)?

And how did Sarah respond to Abraham's response regarding Hagar's response (verse 6)? (I know it's a mess!)

In the end, what happened (verse 6)?

...and Your Heart's Answer

• God obviously had a lot of work to do in Sarah's life to transform her from this finagling, faithless woman into the woman of the Bible who ultimately became known as a model for us all, who (please read these verses for yourself)...

—exhibited a gentle and quiet spirit (1 Peter 3:4),

—trusted in God (1 Peter 3:5),

—walked boldly in God's ways (1 Peter 3:6), and

—qualified as one of the giants of the faith (Hebrews 11:11).

If anything, the six verses that make up this lesson have to do with the *failure* to wait on God to fulfill one of His promises. Here we witness a firsthand look at the trouble that so often results when we fail to wait on God, to trust in Him, and instead take matters into our own hands.

Sarah couldn't wait. Time was the greatest foe to her faith, and so she moved ahead. Unable to wait for the *divine*, she moved ahead with the *devised*. Yes, Sarah clearly failed when it came to "the wait of faith." Instead she took over for God. On her own and in her own way, she tried to help God out, to help God fulfill His promise to Abraham.

• Our Sarah is not alone in her inability to wait on God. Saul, first king of Israel, was another who had the same problem. What did the prophet Samuel tell Saul to do in 1 Samuel 10:8?

However, when Samuel didn't arrive, Saul took matters into his own hands. (Does this sound familiar?) What did Saul do in 1 Samuel 13:8-9?

Immediately, what happened (1 Samuel 13:10)?

As with Sarah, Saul's inability to wait cost dearly. What to-the-point statement did Samuel make to Saul regarding his failure to wait (1 Samuel 13:13)?

• Now for you, my friend. I know it's painful to look at your own past mistakes. But, as you think back on some of these incidents (the really *big* ones, the blunders!), could they just possibly have been avoided if you had only waited? Waited on God? Please explain.

From the Heart

In our instant society we want everything now, don't we? Just think of your own children. How many times do you have to tell them to wait? As God's children, we, too, have a problem with waiting. How many times does God have to tell *you* to wait?

In honor of this lesson—and its invaluable instruction to us about waiting on God—I've created this acrostic on the word *wait*.

W- hat benefit will result if you wait? How many times have you waited on buying an item only to find it on sale later?

A- lways see waiting as an opportunity to trust God (Psalm 27:14).

I- nclude prayer in your daily waiting. Prayer helps match the beat of our hearts to God's metronome. Let Him set the pace and the speed.

T- ime is not an obstacle to God. With the Lord one day is as a thousand years, and a thousand years as one day (2 Peter 3:8).

Seeking the Lost

Genesis 16:7-16

*I'*m not a fiction writer (and, wow!, do I ever admire those who can create stories and keep readers like you and me eagerly turning the pages!). But I do know that one good rule for writing fiction is to drop in little surprises here and there. For instance, one chapter ends, sort of ho-hum, and then you turn the page, and bam! there's a surprise!

Well, that's what's happening right here in Genesis 16. Inserted into the massive lives of Abraham and Sarah, the big-time players in God's arena of faith, is a surprise section on the life of a "nobody," one of "the little people," an obscure pagan servant girl from another country, who became permanently interwoven into the lives of God's great couple of the faith. Unfortunately, this member of the numberless band of nobodies was to witness, partake of, and suffer from the consequences of the dark side, the faithless side, of God's choice twosome. However, the bright side of Hagar's ordeal was witnessing two appearances of God Himself, a privilege very few have experienced!

As we step into this chapter in the life of the poor little nobody, Hagar (whose name, by the way, means "flight"), we also step into Encounter #1 with the Angel of the Lord, Jehovah Himself! Just to get us started, here's a bare-bones outline from Genesis 16:1-6 to bring us up to date on Hagar's story and how we come to find her running from Sarah:

Sarah   *acted*—verse 2

Hagar was   *arrogant*—verse 4

Sarah   *accused* Abraham—verse 5

Sarah was   *angry*—verse 6

God's Input...

1. Read Genesis 16:7-12. Who came after Hagar, and where was she (verse 7)?

   How did He address Hagar (verse 8)?

   And what two questions did He ask Hagar (verse 8)?

   What two clear words of instruction did He have for Hagar (verse 9)?

And what promise did He share with Hagar (verse 10)?

What was Hagar's son's name to be, and what was its meaning (verse 12)?

Describe Hagar's future son (verse 12).

2. Next read Genesis 16:13-16. How did Hagar refer to the Angel of the Lord (verse 13)?

What was Hagar's son named (verse 15)?

And what was Abraham's age at Ishmael's birth (verse 16)?

(Also, remember throughout our study that Sarah is ten years younger than Abraham. This makes her now _____ years old.)

...and Your Heart's Answer

Well, our dear Sarah's walk in the promises of God (as we've been noting) has not been going very well! God had, indeed, promised offspring to Abraham. So we might say that Abraham was "out to lunch" when he failed to consult God before approving Sarah's scheme to involve Hagar. And Sarah was "out of control" as she lashed out at Hagar and mistreated her. In fact, many scholars believe there were not only bursts of temper, but possibly even blows.

But this lesson is about Hagar. So let's take note of Hagar's "walk" also. A few facts will help us out.

> Hagar was probably heading back to her native land of Egypt (Genesis 16:1).

> Hagar was found by the Angel of the Lord on the side of a caravan road, in the midst of Shur, a 150-mile sandy desert between Palestine and Egypt.[20]

> Hagar's son was to be a wild man, literally "a wild ass man," expressing how the wildness of Ishmael and his descendants would resemble that of a wild donkey. He would be rude, turbulent, and a plunderer, roaming and pitching tents in the desert, a man with a ferocious disposition and without friends or loyalties.

> Hagar was privileged to experience God's gracious appearance in this hour of her deep distress. This is the first recorded appearance of the Angel of the Lord, Jehovah Himself. He identifies Himself with Jehovah and speaks and acts with God's authority.

But this running, fleeing woman was not without fault!

• What fault do we see in Hagar in Genesis 16:4?

And what fault do we see in Hagar in Genesis 16:6?

• What does Proverbs 30:21-23 have to say about such a problem?

• This is a good time for an "attitude check" in your own heart, dear one. Is there any person in authority over you whom you despise or resent or resist or hold in contempt? Has pride overtaken you in any of your relationships? Think it through: husband...parent...pastor...employer...friend who has wronged you...sibling?

Ours is to be a walk and a work characterized by service, a walk of submission, "not with eyeservice, as menpleasers, but in sincerity of heart, fearing God" (Colossians 3:22). What does Colossians 3:23 add to this formula for loyal service and humble submission to others?

From the Heart

Do you ever think of yourself as a nobody, my dear reading friend? Or, do you ever think that nobody cares? That nobody knows of your suffering? That nobody is aware of you? That nobody is aware that you've been unfairly mistreated? Do you ever consider yourself to be abandoned and discarded? Neglected or passed over? Do you ever want to just give up?

Well, take heart. Why? Because *God* cares, and, in God's economy, nobody is a nobody! Our God sees. He hears. He notices. And He acts. Therefore, you must never consider yourself to be a nobody in God's eyes!

And our God also seeks. He came looking for Adam and Eve. He came looking for David—yes, David, the "runt" of Jesse's litter of sons, but "the man after God's own heart." He came looking for Saul of Tarsus. And He, the God-who-sees, came looking for Hagar.

Thank God now that He also came looking for *you!* As Jesus Christ reminded Zacchaeus, another of "the little people" and another nobody, "the son of Man has come to seek and to save that which was lost" (Luke 19:10).

Lesson 12

Walking with God

Genesis 17:1-14

*W*hat a privilege it was for my husband to officiate at the weddings of both of our daughters! With the authority of an ordained minister and the tenderness of a father, Jim did what no other person could do in a way and with a heart that no other person could have duplicated. I can still picture him standing at the altar in our church's chapel addressing both girls and their husbands-to-be. And I can still hear him calling for solemn "I will"s and "I do"s from each couple as they entered into the covenant of marriage.

Well, today, my fellow "walking" partner, we have a similar but much more serious covenant taking place. And it, too, called for some sober "I will"s and "I do"s. Let's eavesdrop as God Almighty, El Shaddai, appears to Sarah's husband Abraham and talks with him.

God's Input....

1. First read Genesis 17:1-3. What is the first fact we learn about Abraham (verse 1)?

And how old does that make Sarah, who is ten years Abraham's junior?

To get this scene in proper perspective, realize that it takes place about 13 years after the birth of Ishmael, Abraham's son by Sarah's servant Hagar. Thirteen years have passed between our last lesson and this one and between chapter 16 and chapter 17 of Genesis.

How does God refer to Himself (verse 1)?

Please note that *God Almighty* is a translation of God's name *El Shaddai*. El Shaddai carries the meaning of "God-who-is-sufficient" and of "mountain" as in God is a "rock." It emphasizes God's might over against man's frailty.[21]

What was God's twofold command to Abraham (verse 1)?

And what was God's twofold promise to Abraham if he would obey the commands (verse 2)?

How did Abraham respond to God's appearance and message (verse 3)?

2. Now read Genesis 17:4-8. Up until this encounter with God, Sarah's husband's name has been *Abram*, meaning "exalted father." Now what new name does God give to him, a name meaning "father of a multitude of nations" (verse 5)?

Briefly, what is the content of God's covenant with Abraham and His promises to Abraham (verses 6-8)?

3. Next read Genesis 17:9-14. Now that God has stated His part of the covenant ("As for Me"—verses 4-8), He delineates Abraham's part of the covenant ("As for you"—verses 9-14). What did Abraham's part consist of according to...

Verse 10–

Verse 11–

Verse 12–

Verse 13–

What would happen to those who failed to follow God's condition of circumcision (verse 14)?

For your information, circumcision was not a new rite. It was widespread in the Near East. Here we see God initiating circumcision as a sign of and a seal for the covenant between Himself and Abraham. Circumcision would be the outward sign of an inward heart. It was to be the symbol of at least four commitments: 1) to the covenant; 2) to wholehearted consecration to God; 3) to the casting-off of heathen ways; and 4) to the casting-off of self-will.[22]

...and Your Heart's Answer

- There are broader spiritual implications to God's demand for circumcision that you and I must take to heart. How do Acts 7:8 and Romans 4:11 refer to this rite?

  How does Jeremiah 4:4 describe the true meaning of such a ritual?

  And Deuteronomy 10:16?

  And Colossians 2:11-12?

- Now describe in your own words the heart condition God is seeking in your walk with Him.

From the Heart

As I studied and thought—and prayed!—through this powerful and pivotal passage that reaffirms the Abrahamic

Covenant and points to the ultimate descendant of Abraham, Jesus Christ, in whom all the nations will be blessed, I couldn't help but dwell on these mighty truths:

Person of God—Here God is revealed as El Shaddai, as The Almighty God, as a rock, as God All-bountiful, and as the One who is all-sufficient. By His very nature, El Shaddai encourages us, as one so eloquently writes, "for all the pilgrimage, however long the march, or difficult the route."[23] And by His faithfulness, He works in our lives and fulfills His promises...in His own time and in His own way!

Obedience to God—As with Abraham, we as believers in Jesus Christ are saved unconditionally. But conditionally, as with Abraham, we, too, must *walk* with God in faith and in obedience. We must do whatever God commands...and do it wholeheartedly. God desires no distant or halfhearted association with you and me, dear woman after God's own heart. No, He seeks a wholehearted relationship. God calls us to...

...wholeness in our surrender

...wholeness in our obedience

Promises of God—God promised to give Abraham progeny, power, posterity, property, and a personal relationship. We, too, have been given the "exceedingly great and precious promises" (2 Peter 1:4). Now, let's walk in them with a wholehearted trust in the Person of God and with wholehearted obedience!

 esson 13

Obeying the Lord

I know I've already shared a couple of my favorite hymns in our study, and I just can't resist letting you know about another one, which is probably one of yours, too. Its title pretty much sums up the Christian life and our walk with the Lord. Let's take a minute to enjoy it together.

Trust and Obey
When we walk with the Lord
In the light of His Word
What a glory He sheds on our way!
While we do His good will,
He abides with us still,
And with all who will trust and obey.[24]

Whenever I attempt to characterize Abraham, one word always rushes to my mind—*obedience!* It seems that whenever and whatever God asked of him, Abraham was quick to carry it out. What happened when God asked Abraham to leave his home? "By faith, Abraham obeyed when he was called to go out" (Hebrews 11:8). We have yet to see (later in Lesson 22) God's most severe test of Abraham's faith and Abraham's immediate obedience when "he rose up early in the morning" and went out to obey God (Genesis 22:3).

Right now let's learn of yet another instance of Abraham's obeying the Lord.

God's Input...

1. As we open up this next lesson and passage from God's Word, we see that Sarah is now most definitely involved as God speaks these words to Abraham, "As for Sarai your wife..." (Genesis 17:15). What did God say in the remainder of this verse (verse 15)?

   What promise did God give regarding Sarah in verse 16?

   And what did her future hold (verse 16)?

2. When Abraham heard the good news, what two responses did he give (verse 17)?

   Why was he so astounded (verse 17)?

   And what did he pray regarding Ishmael (verse 18)?

And, in a word, what was God's answer (verse 19)?

God said Isaac instead of Ishmael was to be the child of the covenant. (And, for your information...*Isaac* means "he laughs"!)

3. What was to happen to Ishmael (verse 20)?

Finish verse 21 here: "But...

4. Moved by faith and a desire to be obedient, Abraham immediately followed through on God's covenant command. What did he do (verse 23)?

Who was involved in this act (verses 23 and 26-27)?

...and Your Heart's Answer

Hold on, dear reader (and dear Sarah!)! Things are about to change around Sarah's tent. God has just delivered dazzling news!

• The changes all started with a name change. God changed her name from _____ to _____ (verse 15).

By way of information, Sarah means "princess" and is the feminine form of "prince." This new name emphasized the role she was to play in the future as Abraham's wife, "a mother of nations."

How does God describe the title "mother of nations" (verse 16)?

• God promised a child to Abraham *by Sarah* (verse 16)! She would have the inexpressible (and, in her case, miraculous!) joy of welcoming a son through whom God's covenant promises would be fulfilled. As incredible as it seemed, it was a sure word from the Lord. A son had been promised long ago to Abraham. Now Abraham was, for the first time, informed that it was to be a child of Sarah. How old was the princess Sarah now (verse 17)?

What does Psalm 113:9 say about such a blessing?

• God promised that Sarah would become "a mother of nations" (Genesis 17:16). How numerous were her off-spring to become according to Genesis 22:17?

And speaking of "a mother of nations..."

...back in 1703 a godly woman named Esther Edwards gave birth to a son she named Jonathan. From this woman's son, who would become distinguished as a theologian and preacher, came an amazing line of offspring. More than 400 have been traced, and that number includes 14 college presidents and 100 professors. Another 100 were ministers of the gospel, missionaries, and theological teachers. Still another 100-plus were lawyers and judges, 60 were doctors, and as many more were authors and editors of high rank.[25]

How do you see your mothering, my friend? Is it a bother...or a blessing? Are you committed...or coping? If you're a mother, do you see your role as a meaningful one? Do you faithfully instill God's truth into those little ones in front of you...praying all the while for their little ones...and their little ones...and their little ones? Take a minute to write out a few sentences about your heart and efforts regarding your children. Do you need to make any changes? If so, write out a prayer from your heart to God's.

Yes, the pattern of Sarah's life was about to change dramatically! Drastically! Imagine, being barren until age 90 and then having a baby! But God is on the move, and His plan to reach and bless all the nations is moving toward fulfillment. And our Sarah was to be a key player! Oh, joy!

- God's promises should bring blessing to our lives. And they blessed dear Abraham so deeply that, upon hearing that his Sarah would have a son in her old age (his, too!), Abraham laughed (Genesis 17:17)! It wasn't a laugh of unbelief. No, Abraham had his joy, too! His laugh was one of overwhelming gladness and amazement.

Another man received much the same kind of announcement. That man was Zacharias, a priest whose wife Elizabeth was also barren and past the age of childbearing. Their story is told in Luke 1. When the angel Gabriel appeared to Zacharias with the good news of a baby to be born to him and his Elizabeth, how did Zacharias respond in Luke 1:18?

Now *that*, dear one, was a response of unbelief. No, Abraham's was not a derisive laugh, but rather one of delight. As devotional commentator Matthew Henry remarks, "Even the promises of a holy God, as well as his performances, are the joys of holy souls; there is the joy of faith as well as the joy of fruition."[26]

From the Heart

Drawing from the life of Abraham, I would like to ask you this question: How do you tend to respond to God's commands? Do you *obey* them? Do you follow through wholeheartedly? Do you move out immediately? Or do you wait, dawdle, and *delay* obeying them? I know I'm praying for an obedient heart for myself—and for you, too!

And drawing from the life of Sarah, I would like to ask you this question: How do you tend to respond to God's promises? Do you believe them? Do you embrace them wholeheartedly? And are you able to wait for their fulfillment? Or do you snicker and doubt and question God? I hope and pray you are in the embrace-and-believe category! I hope and pray that you, beloved, are a woman after God's own heart, a woman who walks in all of God's ways and delights in all of God's promises, knowing that...

*E*very promise is built upon four pillars—

—God's justice and holiness, which will not suffer Him to deceive;

—God's grace or goodness, which will not suffer Him to forget;

—God's truth, which will not suffer Him to change; and

—God's power, which makes Him able to accomplish.[27]

esson 14

Receiving Good News

Genesis 18:1-22

I can't begin to count the number of times my dear husband has called me from work to announce, "Well, I've got good news and bad news. Which would you like to hear first?"

And these words sort of describe today's lesson. God had several announcements to make to Sarah and Abraham— one was good news and the other bad news. And so "the LORD appeared" to Abraham one day during Abraham's midday siesta. Do you want to know what the good news was, and what the bad news was? Read on!

God's Input...

1. "Angels unawares." That's how the King James Version of the Bible describes what happened next on the path of

Sarah's life (Hebrews 13:2). Read Genesis 18:1-8. As Abraham lazed in his tent's doorway to catch a faint breeze, what did he see when he raised his eyelids (verse 2)?

And what was his response (verse 2)?

What did he ask of them (verses 4-5)?

How was his request answered (verse 5)?

Now Abraham is on the move! What did he ask of Sarah (verse 6)?

And what was his next act (verse 7)?

In the end Abraham set a sumptuous meal in front of his guests and waited on them.

Note that we are witnessing hospitality that is still true today of the bedouin culture.

2. Now read Genesis 18:9-15 to discover "the good news" and learn a little more about the path of Sarah's life. What question did the three visitors ask of Abraham (verse 9)?

Next, the good news was delivered. What was it (verse 10)?

The happy event was only a year away! Oh, glory! And yet how did Sarah respond (verse 12)?

Perhaps why (verses 11-12)?

3. Verse 13 reveals the identity of one of the guests. Who was He?

What was His question (verse 13)?

And what was His reasoning as he repeated the good news (verse 14)?

Poor Sarah! What was her response...and why (verse 15)?

4. Finally, read Genesis 18:16-22. The "good news" brought exceeding and marvelous joy and light as bright as this cheery noonday encounter. However, the "bad news" now to be revealed paints a dismal and dark picture. In what direction did the three celestial visitors now turn their attention (verse 16) as the pleasantries of a sumptuous meal ended?

Again, who was one of the visitors according to verse 17?

And what was His question (verses 17-18)?

According to God, what is one key role all Christian parents have (verse 19)?

What was going on in Sodom and Gomorrah (verses 20-22)?

And who was in Sodom and Gomorrah (Genesis 13:10-12)?

...and Your Heart's Answer

We noted earlier that old Sarah's life was about to change, and here we read about some of the changes and get some additional insights into the pattern of her daily life and walk. For our purposes, let's focus on three features.

- *Hospitality*—It's true that Sarah and Abraham lived in a desert and probably didn't have a lot of visitors! Maybe that's one reason they seem to have *jumped* and *scurried about* when three visitors appeared one day. However, in their day a person's reputation was connected with their hospitality. Everyone was treated as an honored guest, and food and lodging were freely bestowed.

What does the New Testament have to say about you and the importance of practicing hospitality in 1 Timothy 5:10?

And Hebrews 13:2?

And in 1 Peter 4:9 (and don't forget to note the final words of this verse!)?

Before we move from this important aspect of Christianity (and one which you and I can readily apply), take a few minutes to jot down how these women served others through hospitality:

Rebecca in Genesis 24:23-25–

Rachel in Genesis 29:13-14–

Lydia in Acts 16:15–

Priscilla in 1 Corinthians 16:19–

- *Faith*—"*Is anything too hard for the* LORD?" *Hard* literally means "wonderful," making God's question read, "Is anything too wonderful for the LORD?" Sarah treated God's announcement as incredible! Impossible! Yet what does Luke 1:37 have to tell us on this subject?

Yes, what God proposed was unusual, extraordinary, and beyond the natural. What God was proposing was something *super*natural, something that lay in the realm of God, something that required a miracle—something God was well capable of accomplishing!

- *Parenting*—How do the instructions for fathers in 1 Timothy 3:4 echo God's instructions found in Genesis 18:19?

And Ephesians 6:4?

And what advice does Deuteronomy 6:6-7 offer both mothers and fathers in this vital area of teaching their children about the things of the Lord?

From the Heart

"Is anything too hard for the LORD?" We've already seen how Sarah apparently answered this question. Unfortunately, there was something she thought was indeed too hard for the Lord. In a faithless moment, Sarah appears to have concluded that it was too hard for the Lord to enable her old, worn out, withered, and ready-to-fall-apart body (that's the literal meaning here) to conceive a child, give birth to a child, and nurture a child. How wrong she was!

Now, how would *you* answer that question, dear one? "*Is* anything too hard for the LORD?"

Interceding for Others

Genesis 18:23-33

I have to say, from my heart to yours, that nothing in life (outside of my relationship with the Lord, of course!) compares in importance—or emotion—to what's going on in the lives of those in my own family. It's been my experience that when things are not quite right in the family, or when some family member is going through some difficulty, everything else fades in importance. I know when my father was dying of cancer and I spent almost a full year assisting him, other things dwindled in significance. I cared little about world news, politics, the latest Hollywood gossip, the newest fads, etc. The same thing happened when one of my daughters gave birth to a child with a physical disability. Somehow the other affairs in life just did not matter so much at those times of crisis. My heart was elsewhere!

I can tell you also, from my own life and heart, that I carry my family members nearest and dearest to my heart when it comes to the matter of prayer. When it comes to my family, Paul's words say it all—"I have you in my heart" (Philippians 1:7).

Today, in a tender scene from the life and heart of Sarah's husband Abraham, we witness such familial care and concern. There's trouble a'brewin'! Trouble in Abraham's clan! And does he ever show us the right way to handle it!!!

God's Input....

1. Let's review. Our last lesson left off with the "good news" of God's good news/bad news announcements—both having to do with family. Briefly, what was the good news (Genesis 18:10)?

2. Next God turned His attention toward the "bad news," toward Sodom and Gomorrah. His concern indicated that there was a problem with the place where Sarah and Abraham's nephew Lot lived. How did Abraham react (verse 22)?

3. Now read Genesis 18:23-33 and try to grasp the progression of this instructive conversation between Abraham and the Lord by filling in the following information:

   What was Abraham's opening question of the Lord (verse 23)?

   And Abraham's hypothetical question (verse 24)?

And Abraham's appeal to God on the basis of His character (verse 25)?

What was God's answer (verse 26)?

On and on Abraham went, calling upon God's nature to spare the righteous! What number of people did Abraham ask God to spare in these verses?

Verse 28–   Verse 31–

Verse 29–   Verse 32–

Verse 30–

Briefly, in every case, what was God's answer?

A little P.S.—God already knew, as we'll soon see, that there weren't even *ten* righteous people in Sodom and Gomorrah!

...and Your Heart's Answer

This passage, dear one, once again reveals to us the character of Sarah's husband. He was a man after God's own heart...and a man who loved his family deeply! And this passage also remarkably and clearly reveals the character of *God!* It also teaches us about intercessory prayer.

- *About the Person of God*—Here God is...

  ...fair—He checked out the situation in Sodom and Gomorrah before acting.

  ...patient—with Abraham's asking, with Lot, and with Sodom and Gomorrah.

  ...merciful—He would spare...and had spared.

  ...just—He punishes sin.

  ...approachable—He allowed Abraham to talk with Him, to ask of Him, to "bargain" with Him.

- *About prayer*—If God is approachable, then we can approach God! In your own words, what does Abraham's language when speaking to God indicate about the manner in which he approached God (see verses 27, 30, 32)? Can you think of three or four single words that describe Abraham's solicitation of the Lord?

What does Proverbs 15:8 have to say about prayer?

And James 5:16?

As another has noted about prayer...and about Abraham,

> *I*ntercessory prayer always brings out the best in men. Their unselfish concern for others shines like a beautiful jewel. In pleading with the Lord, Abraham clearly demonstrated genuine love and concern. And he experienced anew the friendship of God in His willingness to counsel with him and grant him a special revelation before the doom fell.[28]

• Beloved, who are the "others" you intercede in prayer for? Here we witness Abraham interceding for his family. Who are the family members you regularly bring before God in prayer? And how regularly and faithfully do you do that? Do you need to make any changes in your prayer life or on your prayer list? Answer these questions now.

• Also, do you agree with the statement made above, "Intercessory prayer always brings out the best in men"? Explain your answer (and hopefully from firsthand experience!).

• Is your intercessory prayer life and unselfish concern for others shining like a beautiful jewel? Jot down some new intentions and habits that will brighten up this beautiful jewel!

From the Heart

Since God promises to answer our prayers, let's then focus on "the practice of prayer" in this section. What additional guidelines and promises regarding prayer does God's Word give us to encourage us in prayer and to assist us in a more profitable prayer life? (And don't forget to notice God's conditions for realizing the promises!)

Matthew 7:7-8–

Matthew 21:22–

Mark 11:23-24–

John 15:7–

James 4:2-3–

1 John 3:22–

1 John 5:14-15–

Are you living a life that is pleasing to the Lord, dear one? Are you abiding in Him? Are you asking according to His will as revealed in His Holy Word? And are you diligent in asking, seeking, and knocking? Are you following in the pattern Abraham set for us of passionately interceding for your special others?

*L*esson 16

Rescuing Lot…Again!

Genesis 19:1-14

*I*t's Lot again! Sarah and Abraham's nephew. You know, the one whose herdsmen fought with Uncle Abraham's herdsmen? The one who chose the luscious, fertile plains of Sodom and Gomorrah, leaving gracious Abraham to fend for himself with the drier foothills of Canaan as grazing land for his cattle?

We—you and I and Sarah and Abraham and God—all knew that Lot made a bad choice when he chose to go to Sodom. A dangerous choice. The wrong choice. For, as the Bible explained, "the men of Sodom were exceedingly wicked and sinful against the LORD" (Genesis 13:13).

Well, dear friend, today we observe firsthand that it was a *disastrous decision!* All I can say is, be prepared! It's an awful scene. And it's hard to read. You may even be tempted to wonder why such vile debauchery appears on the pages of God's Holy Word. Yet, as one writer remarks,

> ...God inspired Moses to record at length all that followed Lot's decision, because He wants us to be aware of the results of self-centered decisions. Though these details are rather graphic—the Bible is an honest book—they serve as a serious warning to any person who is tempted to play with fire. You cannot escape without getting burned.[29]

God's Input...

When it came to "family," Lot was all that Sarah and Abraham had. Sure, they had left other family behind when they departed from Ur of the Chaldees (Genesis 11:27-31). And yes, their lives would once again intertwine (Genesis 24). But we can just imagine the place Lot held in the hearts of dear old childless Sarah and Abraham! Let's see what next unfolds in their beloved nephew's life.

1. Read Genesis 19:1-3. Who approached Sodom, and where do we find Lot (verse 1)?

   What did Lot offer the two angels (verses 2-3)?

2. Now read Genesis 19:4-5. What happened next?

   To clarify, these men "sought homosexual relations with the visitors."[30]

3. Next read Genesis 19:6-9 (if you can stomach it!). In order to protect his two celestial guests, what incomprehensible(!) solution did Lot suggest (verse 8)?

What was the attitude of the men of Sodom toward Lot, and how did they respond to his suggestion (verse 9)?

4. Now read Genesis 19:10-11. How did the angels save Lot's life (verse 10)?

And what did they do to the men of the city (verse 11)?

5. Finally, read Genesis 19:12-14. The angels now turn their attention to Lot and his family. What are their instructions to Lot, and why (verses 12-13)?

What was the attitude of Lot's sons-in-law toward Lot and his message (verse 14)?

...and Your Heart's Answer

- What happened to Lot and his family speaks loudly to us about *our* walk, about the direction of *our* life, and the difference *our* decisions make in *our* walk and the path of *our* life. These observations regarding Lot's "walk" come to us from Dr. Gene Getz of Dallas Theological Seminary. I'll note here and now only those results that apply to Genesis 19:1-14, our text for this lesson. Then we'll look at the other "results" in our next study.

The Results of Lot's Decision (Genesis 19)

— Lot was subject to great harassment and
demands (verses 4-7,9).

— Lot lost all sense of moral values (verse 8).

— Lot lost his influence over those closest to
him (verse 14).[31]

- What do these scriptures have to say about making
"right" decisions?

Psalm 37:4-5–

Proverbs 3:5-6–

Proverbs 16:3–

Jeremiah 17:9-10–

James 1:5–

James 4:17–

- We know what Lot did and where he went wrong, but
why read about it? Because God speaks to us through
His Word and Lot's example. So as women after God's
own heart, let's take the wisdom from the above verses
to heart and do a heart check:

—*Who* are your best friends, the people you spend most
of your time with? And *what* kind of people are they?

Do you see their influence on you as godly or ungodly? Please explain your answer.

—*Where* do you tend to spend your time, to "hang out"? *What* do you see and witness and hear when you are there? Is the influence on you godly or ungodly? Again, please explain your answer.

• When Lot made his disastrous decision, he *looked*, he *longed*, and he *left*—but his was the wrong formula. Now take a look at a better formula from God's Word:

> *W*hen you are making a decision...
>
> ...*look* to God through His Word and through prayer (Psalm 63:1).
>
> ...*long* for the things of God versus the things of this world (1 John 2:15-17).
>
> ...*leave* the things of this world and set your affection on things above (Colossians 3:1-2).

Note here a decision you need to make. Then consider how God's *looking*, *longing*, and *leaving* formula would make a difference and prevent you from making a disastrous decision. Then purpose to follow God's formula instead of Lot's!

From the Heart

Let's not forget that it was Abraham who had pleaded with God to preserve Lot and his family. And Genesis 19 shows God graciously—and mightily...and miraculously!—rescuing the rascal Lot.

So, what can you and I learn from Abraham, and what can you and I do for and about our own erring family members? Put these principles to work for your kinfolk:

> *Pray*—Abraham spoke often with God about the things on his heart, and we can be sure that his nearest and dearest relative, Lot, was on his heart! Speak to God regularly about your loved ones.

> *Petition*—Abraham beseeched and appealed to God on behalf of Lot and his family, and you must do the same. Your part (as we've been learning) is to ask. The answer is up to God.

> *Persevere*—Abraham never gave up, on Lot or on God. Neither must you.

> *Persuade*—Take every opportunity to give good advice, even warning when you must and when it's appropriate.

> *Passionately love*—Abraham, in spite of how he was treated by Lot, never evidenced any bitterness, resentment, or ill will toward Lot. Instead we see gracious, passionate love, a love that you can, with the Lord's help, duplicate.

Lesson 17

Sowing...and Reaping

Genesis 19:15-38

Like a drama, the biblical account of Sarah and Abraham's nephew Lot's life is moving toward a climax. Masterfully, the background has been laid. The characters have been well developed. The plot has been leading up to some catastrophe as two angels arrive on the scene. Things are in motion. Emotions are heightened. We can sense trouble, action, and some kind of conclusion...soon! Things just can't continue as they are. *Something* must happen! Indeed, all of our senses are waiting for it, for *something!* I've heard others call such dramatic tension "waiting for the other shoe to drop." What will it be? And when?

God's Input....

1. Poor Sarah. And poor Abraham. As I just said, the scene is now set. We now know what Lot's poor decisions led to and the kind of place he lived in. And neither is very nice! No, the path of Lot's life has taken some nasty turns. In New Testament terms, "righteous Lot" (2 Peter 2:7-8) is reaping what he's sown! Galatians 6:7 puts it in clear language: "Do not be deceived. God is not mocked; for whatever a man sows, that he will also reap."

Read Genesis 19:15-22 to see what happened "when the morning dawned." What was the command given to Lot by his angelic visitors (verse 15)?

How well did Lot heed the angels' instructions (verse 16)?

What did the angels do to save Lot's family (verse 16)?

And how is God described (verse 16)?

What were the three specific instructions Lot was given (verse 17)?

What "excuses" did Lot present for not following the instructions (verses 18-20)?

And what was the angel's gracious reply (verses 21-22)?

2. Now read Genesis 19:23-29. What happened as soon as Lot's group entered Zoar—meaning "little" (verses 23-25)?

And what happened to Lot's wife (verse 26)?

When Abraham looked toward Sodom and Gomorrah, what did he see (verses 27-28)?

What does verse 29 tell us about the relationship Abraham had with God?

3. I hate to ask this of you, but we must now read Genesis 19:30-38. *Who* is now living *where*, and *why* (verse 30)?

In as few words as possible, what happened in verses 31-36?

What are the names of the children who came out of this confusing and distasteful scene (verses 37-38)?

...and Your Heart's Answer

• No, this passage of Scripture is not about Sarah. It's about her nephew Lot. But it does contain messages for you and me about the pattern of our walk and warnings to us from the pattern of Lot's walk.

This is the last Old Testament reference to Lot. What an ending to the account of a life! Look at Galatians 6:7 again and write it out here. (You should also memorize it!)

Consider Lot's life and what he had "sown." Briefly relate the mistakes he made. You may want to review Lesson 6 and revisit Genesis 13. Then look at the following list continued from our previous lesson on Lot's downfall.

The Results of Lot's Decision (Genesis 19)—*continued*

—Lot lost his will to do what was right (verse 16).

—Lot took advantage of God's grace (verses 19-23).

—Lot lost his most prized possession—his wife (verse 26).

—Lot committed sin with his own daughters (verse 30-38).[32]

- Look at Psalm 1. Chart the behaviors of the man (or woman) who is blessed (verses 1-3) and the one who is cursed (verses 4-5).

Blessed is...   *Cursed is...*

- Now spend some time considering the pattern of your walk. Are you faithfully looking to God and making choices that lead to God's blessing, as Psalm 1 remarks?

Or, are you sowing seed that is reaping havoc, confusion, and unsavory fruit? Be honest, and be specific.

From the Heart

Well, how did you do, dear woman after God's own heart? A look in the mirror is always sobering and revealing, isn't it? As women we often check out our looks in a mirror...but more important is to check out our heart! Are you doing well, at least today? Then *thank God* for His marvelous grace! Are you failing? Then *turn away* from the behaviors that are sowing a crop of failures. And we can all use improvement, so *take to heart* God's instruction to delight in Him and in His Word (Psalm 1:2).

And then, as verse 3 of Psalm 1 promises, *whatever you do shall prosper.* In other words, you will enjoy deep-seated joy and contentment in God as He brings you to maturity. You will become more and more "rooted" in eternal realities. Constant vitality is assured and ultimate "success" is certain because you are putting your trust firmly in God.

Now that's a worthy walk!

Lesson 18

Failing in Faith

One step forward, two steps back. Or is it two steps forward, one step back? Or is it, as author and teacher Chuck Swindoll entitled his book on the subject of spiritual growth, *Three Steps Forward, Two Steps Back?* I certainly hope the pattern and progress of our faith is at least this positive!

Personally, I'm a "journaller." I'm not what I call a "morbid journaller" who tries to capture forever every feeling and failure. But I do try at each day's end to make note of the general tenor of the day. I always thank God for His grace whenever I'm able to report a "good" day, and I always ask for His forgiveness and His help whenever I must admit to a "bad" day. I'm not talking about days with or without trouble. No, Jesus *promised* that we would have tribulation (John 16:33); trials are a fact of life (James 1:2). I'm talking about days and incidents that I did or did not handle God's way, those instances where I failed or succeeded (and that's again by His grace) to walk in His wisdom and His ways.

Well, we don't know whether Abraham was a journaller or not, but we do know that Moses, the author of the book of Genesis, was a man who wrote things down. And what he has to record for us in this lesson is definitely not to Abraham's honor! Indeed, we read of Abraham, the great hero of the faith, the father of faith, lapsing into some of his old ways. Let's look at the account of a deflection from the pathway of faith on the part of this man of faith.

God's Input....

1. Before we head into this new lesson about yet another journey into faithlessness and scheming that Sarah and Abraham took, review Genesis 12:10-20. In two or three sentences, capsulize what happened in this scene.

2. Now read Genesis 20:1-8. Be sure to consult your map on page 153. What's happening (verse 1)?

   And what did Abraham do that put Sarah at risk (verse 2)?

   If you remember, Genesis 12:17 began, "But the LORD...." How does Genesis 20:3 begin?

3. Please take note that this is a *miracle!* Once again, we witness God coming to the rescue of dear Sarah. What did God say to Abimelech, the king of Gerar (verse 3)?

And how did Abimelech respond to God's announcement (verses 4-5)?

How does Abimelech portray himself (verse 5)?

Did God agree or disagree with Abimelech's self-description (verse 6)?

In fact, what does God say *His* role in this scene of Abimelech's deception by Abraham was (verse 6)?

4. What were God's final instructions to Abimelech (verse 7)?

How is Abraham described to Abimelech (verse 7)?

It's important to note that a prophet "stood in a peculiar relation to the Lord. He had access to God, was protected by divine power, received special revelation, and was obligated to speak for God the message he had received."[33]

How did Abimelech respond to God's instructions (verse 8)?

What was the general tone in Abimelech's household (verse 8)?

...and Your Heart's Answer

"Why, why, why?," we are tempted to query! Haven't we been down this road before, dear Sarah and Abraham?! And was *nothing* learned?! Here you are, Abraham, a *prophet*, one who is "protected by divine power," acting in fear, faithlessness, and foolishness! Oh, will you never learn?!

But we mustn't be too hard on this faltering couple. For, honestly, haven't you been guilty of making the same mistake twice? I know I certainly have!

But still, we do wonder. The pattern of faith that Abraham had established in the intervening years between Incident #1 (reported in Genesis 12) and Incident #2 (reported here in Genesis 20) seems to be broken. And at the same time, the pattern of faithlessness in this one area of lying for the sake of self-preservation seems to be ingrained. Here are a few facts that make this second breach of faith, Incident #2, this relapse, doubly alarming.

Promise (see Genesis 18:10,14)—On the brink of the appearance of the promised child, the promise from God of a child through Sarah is put in jeopardy. Why? Because of fear. For the sake of personal safety.

Premeditation (see Genesis 20:5)—Here God's privileged prophet exhibits premeditated deceit. His lie was deliberate and cunning.

Pain (see Genesis 20:4-7)—Abimelech, a man of great integrity, suffered needless pain and was put at risk by such uncalled-for conniving on Sarah and Abraham's part.

• Sarah and Abraham failed in their faith. What do these scriptures teach us about faith and making mistakes?

   Psalm 86:11–

   Romans 14:23–

   James 1:5-8–

• Now for a few questions for you and me. Rate your usual behavior, or your "trust quotient." Briefly explain your answers:

   You probably believe and trust in the existence of God, but do you trust in His loving care?

   Do you trust God to hear your prayers and to guide you?

   Are you convinced that God's way—His plan—is always best?

   Do you tend to faithfully seek God's leading on a daily basis...or are there lapses?

   Are you generally steady as a rock, firm on the foundation of a solid trust in God...or do you tend to be restless and unsettled? Give some details here of recent opportunities to trust the Lord.

From the Heart

I wish I could ask these questions to your face and learn a little about your life, my friend. Oh, what joy it would be to talk of the Lord together, to revel in His promises, and to pray together! But, for now, look to these "promises" which relate to the questions asked above, and put them into practice in your walk with the Lord.

Psalm 23:1–

Psalm 23:3–

Psalm 62:7–

Psalm 62:8–

Psalm 68:19–

Now, dear one, which promise and practice will you put to work in your life today?

esson 19

Weaving a Masterpiece

Genesis 20:9-18

One of my favorite illustrations that I like to use when I share about the goodness of God has to do with the threads that a weaver uses to weave a beautiful tapestry. The point of the imagery is that the underside of a weaving appears to be merely a mess of knotted and tangled yarns. Yet on the upperside—the weaver's side—a masterpiece is taking shape.

As the message of this picture is driven home to us as women after God's own heart, it reminds us that even though we may not understand or appreciate the confusing pattern of our lives from *our* side of things, God is in control. He knows what He is doing. And from *His* side, the silken threads of our lives are being worked into something lovely and clear—something truly magnificent—something truly worthy to hang in the halls of heaven.

Today, dear one, you and I have the opportunity to look at the tangled mess that sometimes characterized Sarah and Abraham's life, and at the same time to see what God, The Divine Weaver, does to weave the mess into a masterpiece. Let's watch as God goes to work on the life of His patriarch and friend, Abraham, and his wife, Sarah.

God's Input...

In our last lesson, you and I wondered, "Why, why, why?" Well, in this lesson someone else is asking "Why, why, why?" of Abraham. It's Abimelech, king of Gerar. If you'll remember, Abraham had deceived Abimelech and lied about the fact that Sarah was his wife. But God intervened and saved the day! And now it's Abimelech's turn!

1. Read Genesis 20:9-18 and follow along this outline.

Rebuked—What three questions did Abimelech ask of Abraham (verses 9-10)?

For your information..."Abimelech's three questions... make it clear that Abraham had only asked himself *What will this do for me?*, stifling the reflections *What will it do to them?*, *What do they deserve?*, and *What are the facts?*"[34]

How did Abraham reply (verse 11)?

And how did he explain his actions (verse 12)?

Restored—What did Abimelech restore to Abraham (verse 14)?

Rained upon—What did Abimelech bestow and lavish and rain upon Sarah and Abraham (verses 14 and 16)?

Reassured—What did Abimelech assure Abraham was available to him (verse 15)?

2. In return, what did Abraham, the prophet, do for Abimelech (verse 17)?

What had evidently happened to the women in Abimelech's household and why (verses 17-18)?

How was Abraham's prayer answered (verse 17)?

...and Your Heart's Answer

• For whatever reason (submission? agreement? fear?), Sarah went along with Abraham's decision to lie about their relationship. Their act meant that, once again, Sarah was taken into the harem of a pagan king. Once again, she was used to secure Abraham's well-being and physical safety.

Nevertheless, God (once again!) came to the rescue of the mother-to-be of the promised seed. Copy here the words from your Bible that were spoken by Abimelech to Sarah in Genesis 20:16.

Note that the true meaning of these words is that the gifts "will preclude all criticism." In other words, her name was cleared.[35]

- This whole scene is a mess, isn't it? And yet God set about to bring some good out of it, to make something beautiful of it. Abraham was saved, preserved, instructed, blessed, and freed (departing, we hope, a wiser man!). Abimelech was saved, preserved, cleared, and blessed. Sarah was saved, preserved, cleared, blessed, and freed. And the promised seed was saved, preserved, and...well, we'll just have to wait until our next lesson for more on this subject!

Write out Romans 8:28 here and tell how you see God at work here in Sarah and Abraham's walk with Him.

What does Psalm 34:8 have to say about the goodness of God?

And Nahum 1:7?

And what does 2 Peter 2:9 tell us about the Lord?

- As we leave this lesson, what qualities can you emulate from the life of Abimelech?

From the Heart

Now, think about what you are presently going through in your own life. What problems are you facing? What challenges trouble you most? Does the pattern of your life look knotted, tangled, and twisted? Unintelligible? Unnecessary? Do things seem to be a mess?

Well, dear sister-of-Sarah, don't forget about "The Divine Weaver"!

The Divine Weaver

My life is but a weaving
Between my Lord and me;
I cannot choose the colors
He worketh steadily.

Oftimes He weaveth sorrow
And I, in foolish pride,
Forget that He seeth the upper,
And I the under side.

Not till the loom is silent
And the shuttles cease to fly,
Shall God unroll the canvas
And explain the reason why.

The dark threads are as needful
In the Weaver's skillful hand,
As the threads of gold and silver
In the pattern He has planned.[36]

Lesson 20

Waiting, Wondering, and Wandering

Genesis 21:1-13

aiting. Wondering. Wandering. Does it ever seem like your life is made up of these three activities? I can think of a few times in my own life when I waited...and wondered...and wandered. I well remember waiting, like Sarah, for a baby...waiting for Jim to finish a decade of theological training....waiting to hear if Book #1 was well enough received to merit a Book #2...waiting for a doctor's appointment while sensing something was physically wrong inside...waiting on three occasions beside the bed of a loved one who was soon to be with Jesus...wondering when God was going to do something about a person, an issue, or a decision on hold...and wandering as a missionary, living in nine different places in one year. I'm sure you have your own tales to tell in these three faith-producing categories!

119

Waiting, wondering, and *wandering* are three words that also clearly describe what's been going on in the life of Sarah and Abraham for the past 25 years. The suspense has been building since Genesis 12:2 when God first promised descendants to Abraham...even though his wife Sarah was barren (Genesis 11:30).

And so the waiting began.

And the wondering commenced.

And the wandering (sometimes into trouble!) became a lifestyle.

But finally, in the fullness of time (*God's* time) and through a miracle (*God's* method), the tired, old (and literally worn-out) couple welcomed a son!

And you and I, too, are the beneficiaries of this seemingly overdue birth of a little baby. Why? Because every covenant prediction was to have divine fulfillment through this son of Abraham. Abraham's baby, who preceded the holy infant Jesus, was God's gift to the world.

Exactly how did it happen?

God's Input...

1. Read Genesis 21:1-8. What two things did the Lord do in verse 1?

   And what happened to Sarah (verse 2)? (And don't forget to note *when* this happened!)

2. Now for Abraham—What name did he give the child (verse 3)? And why (Genesis 17:19)?

   Remember the name Isaac means..."he laughs."

What else did Abraham do (verse 4)? And why?

How old was Abraham when this son was born (verse 5)?

3. Back to Sarah. Describe Sarah's sentiments according to verses 6 and 7, and then read my own thoughts regarding Sarah's "Season of Joy."

> *The* desert tent rang with sounds of joy! Sarah could not contain her gladness as she held her promised son. It was a season of joyous celebration. Sarah's shameful barrenness had ended (Genesis 11:29). Finally—*finally!*—after 25 years, after hearing the promise again and again, after a visit from God and two angels (Genesis 18:1,2), little Isaac, pink and wrinkled, was born to the aged and wrinkled—but laughing—parents, Abraham and Sarah....
>
> This definitely was an occasion for joy. Isaac was the child of her own body, the child of her old age, the child of God's promise, the fruit of tested faith, the gift of God's grace, and the heaven-appointed heir. So Sarah sang a jubilant song of pure joy, the first-recorded cradle hymn of a mother's thankfulness and delight.[37]

4. Now read Genesis 21:8-13. Something happened to Sarah's joy. What did she see (verse 9), and when did it occur (verse 8)?

Note now...

Sarah's request (verse 10)–

Abraham's response (verse 11)–

God's advice and why (verse 12)–

God's promise (verse 13)–

...and Your Heart's Answer

I well remember attending a Bible study with my husband and listening as the teacher suggested that we each make a chart of our spiritual walk with God. We were to note the highs and the lows, the key people and points of interest, the twists and the turns of our walk with God. Well, both Jim and I did that exercise. And it was quite revealing. In fact, I highly recommend that you do the same. It will most definitely bring the truths and promises of Romans 8:28-29 home to you!

Today we want to notice a few of the directions of dear Sarah's walk with God. Of course, the joyous event before us is like a bomb bursting in air! A literal firework, exploding in all its brilliant, miraculous glory! But what did the path leading up to this joyous display look like? Note what these scriptures remind us of regarding Sarah's waiting, wondering, and wandering:

Genesis 11:30–   Genesis 15:4–

Genesis 12:2–   Genesis 17:19–

Genesis 12:7–   Genesis 18:10–

Genesis 13:15–

And all of this spanned 25 years! These were years of waiting and wondering and wandering...and trusting in the promises of God.

From the Heart

However, true to His promise—and in His own time and in His own way—God gave a baby boy to Sarah and Abraham. God did as He had promised...and He always does. And He did it in His own time—the perfect time! Isaac was born right on schedule—not a second, a day, or a decade (or a quarter-century!) late! God delights in the impossible. Indeed, it's His specialty. As someone has well said, "doing the impossible is everyday business for God."

For what are you waiting, dear one? And are you having any doubts? Even those of great faith may sometimes have doubts. Sarah did. And Abraham did. But, *while* you are waiting (and wondering and wandering!), *while* God seems to be promising the impossible, *while* life seems to be on hold, if you begin to doubt God's leading, do what Sarah and Abraham did.

Step One–   Focus on God and His commitment to fulfill His promises.

Step Two–   Follow God in obedience.

And I would add...

Step Three–   Function. By this I mean stay busy. Be pro-
ductive. Make sure you are moving for-
ward on worthwhile projects. Involve
yourself in the lives of other people. Be a
giving person. "Work out" your faith while
you "work on" your faith by patiently
waiting.

And then one day, beloved, on God's appointed day and
in God's unique way, what once lay in the realm of faith
will be made real. That which was promised will become
reality. And what a glorious day that will be!

esson 21

Sending Hagar Away

Genesis 21:14-34

A word of caution: Before we set about to get to the bottom of the when's and why's of the text, we must never forget that Hagar is a special woman in the Bible. Why? Because she experienced *two* encounters with God Himself! Yes, God in His goodness and faithfulness kept His eye on Hagar, a poor, mistreated, single mom, and on her teenage son. Read Genesis 21:14-21. Then read my words on Hagar.

> *A*s the utter darkness of Hagar's impending death immobilized her to a point of faithlessness, fear, and futility, God's sun of promise began its brilliant ascent. Truly, God's mercies and compassion fail not. They are new every morning (Lamentations 3:22-23)—and so are His promises!...

But Hagar's emergency became God's opportunity. Through the blindness of fear and the blur of hopelessness, Hagar found herself gazing at fresh, rising hope. It was a miracle! From the heavens, God's voice sounded forth His blessed assurance: "I will make him a great nation." Yes, there was hope for tomorrow! And, as God had promised, Hagar lived to see Ishmael grow up, marry, and become the ruler of a great nation (Genesis 21:20, 21; Genesis 25:12-18).[38]

God's Input...

About 16 or 17 years have passed since Round 1 of the "cat fight" between Sarah and her maid Hagar in Genesis 16. If you'll remember, Sarah's makeshift plan for a son included giving Hagar to her husband. Sure enough, Hagar conceived. And her swelling abdomen caused her pride to also swell. Soon Hagar looked with contempt on Sarah, who ordered her out. The intervention of the Lord brought Hagar back to Sarah's home, where Ishmael was later born.

And now, all these years later, we witness Round 2 between Sarah and Hagar. Today Sarah's path involves the expulsion of "the bondwoman" (Genesis 21:10; Galatians 4:30).

Scene 1: Hagar's removal.

1. Review Genesis 21:8-13. Then read Genesis 21:14. What did Abraham do?

2. Now read Genesis 21:15-21. Where are Hagar and Ishmael (verse 14)?

What happened to the food and water supply (verse 15)?

And what was happening to Hagar and Ishmael (verse 16)?

3. How does verse 17 begin?

What were the angel's words to Hagar (verse 17)?

And what were his instructions to Hagar (verse 18)?

And what was his promise to Hagar (verse 18)?

And what was his provision for Hagar and Ishmael (verse 19)?

Note that Hagar's cry was one without hope. It was Ishmael's voice that God harkened to—not Hagar's. His was the cry that brought help! Why? Because of God's promise to Abraham (see Genesis 17:20 and 21:13). And don't forget—the meaning of Ishmael is "God hears" (Genesis 16:11)!

4. How does Hagar and Ishmael's story end (verses 20-21)?

Scene 2: Abraham's pact with Abimelech.

1. There's one more scene here in Genesis 21. Read verses 22-34 and pinpoint Beersheba on your map. What was the cause of this dispute (verse 25), and how did it end (verse 27)?

   What promise do we see being fulfilled here from Genesis 12:2?

   What observation does Abimelech make regarding Abraham's relationship with God in Genesis 21:22?

2. Finally Abraham calls on the Lord. What name does he use (verse 33)?

...and Your Heart's Answer

Regarding Scene 1: Hagar's removal.

• Whether we always appreciate it or not, God is faithful. In the case of Sarah, she may not have appreciated (if, indeed, she even knew about it!) God's care for Hagar and her wild son Ishmael. But what had God promised Abraham in Genesis 17:20?

And what had God promised Hagar in Genesis 16:10?

- Behold the Lord, in His utter faithfulness! As I said, whether we like it or not, whether we care for His ways or not, God *is* faithful. We love it when He's faithful to us. But, dear one, how do you fare when His faithfulness is extended to someone you don't care for, or someone you consider to be unrighteous and undeserving of God's attention? What light do these scriptures shed on this topic?

Exodus 33:19–

Proverbs 24:17-18–

Matthew 5:45–

Regarding Scene 2: Abraham's pact with Abimelech. Abraham had been down this road before! First he and his nephew Lot had been through "a land war," and Abraham had taken the initiative to settle the conflict (Genesis 13). And here in Genesis 21, when trouble arose, these two noble men—Abraham and Abimelech—set about to settle it. Not only did they straighten things out and resolve the disturbance, but they also entered into a covenant with one another.

- How do you handle trouble, my friend? Share the lessons you can learn from these two masters. Then read my own conclusions drawn from how these two handled conflict resolution:

✔ Don't avoid the problem (verses 22-24).

✔ Describe it plainly (verse 25).

✔ Discuss it fully (verse 26).

✔ Deal with it successfully (verse 27).

✔ Declare God's working in your life (verse 33).

✔ Determine to be a peacemaker (verse 34).

Regarding Beersheba (verse 31), it became home base for both Abraham and Isaac. And regarding the Everlasting God (*El Olam*—the God of eternity), Abraham, the patriarch, "would soon march off the map of history, but his God, the unchangeable, Eternal One would remain."[39] Indeed, the Everlasting God, who was before all worlds, will be, even when time and days shall be no more!

From the Heart

We've seen God's faithfulness to Sarah and Abraham and Isaac. But I thought this would be a good place to remember again God's faithfulness to the outcast woman and mother Hagar and her son Ishmael. Here's the end of the devotional thoughts that opened this lesson:

*A*re you enjoying the blazing glory of the many precious promises God gives you in Scripture, hope-filled promises for all your tomorrows? What wonderful promises from Him are you counting on? Thank God for this handful of glistening promises from His vast treasure house of hope:

1. *His constant presence to cheer and to guide.* "I am with you always" (Matthew 28:20).

2. *A new body.* He "will transform our lowly body that it may be conformed to His glorious body" (Philippians 3:21).

3. *A life without sorrow or pain.* "God will wipe away every tear from their eyes; there shall be no more death, nor sorrow, nor crying. There shall be no more pain" (Revelation 21:4).

4. *Eternal life in His gracious presence.* "I give them eternal life, and they shall never perish" (John 10:28).

5. *Rest for your soul.* "Come to Me, all you who labor and are heavy laden, and I will give you rest" (Matthew 11:28).[40]

Now, beloved, which one of these precious promises does your weary soul most need today?

Lesson 22

Willing to Sacrifice All

Genesis 22:1-14

We delight in glibly talking and gushing about loving God. But do we really know what it means to "love" God at all costs? To be willing to sacrifice all in obedience to God— even father and mother, spouse and children, brothers and sisters, yes, even life itself (Luke 14:26)?

Talk is one thing. But action—the true test of love—is quite another. As 1 John 3:18 reminds us, "My little children, let us not love in word or in tongue, but in deed and in truth."

Today's lesson in the life of Sarah and Abraham, which now includes their beloved and long-awaited miracle-child Isaac, is a sobering study on what it means to truly love God. In a word, it means *obedience*, at all costs.

Let's look now and learn what love and faith and obedience and a willingness to sacrifice are all about.

God's Input....

Where was Sarah during these events? We don't know. The Bible doesn't say. Did she even know what was going on? Again, the Bible doesn't say. Regardless of her involvement, these events took place in the lives of her dear husband, Abraham, and their precious son, Isaac. And we can be sure that no one's life was ever quite the same afterward!

1. Read Genesis 22:1-8. What does verse 1 say God was doing?

   What was His command to Abraham (verse 2)?

   How did Abraham respond to such a command (verse 3)?

   As Abraham and Isaac separated from the rest of their party, what did Abraham say to them (verse 5)?

   What does Hebrews 11:17-19 reveal about Abraham's expectation?

   And what had God promised Abraham in Genesis 21:12?

2. Next Isaac had a question. What was it (verse 7)?

   And what was Abraham's answer (verse 8)?

3. Before we move on, a little information and a few insights will help to set the scene:

— *God tested Abraham* (verse 1)—This was not a temptation to sin, but it was a trial that gave Abraham an opportunity to further develop His faith.

— *Moriah* (verse 2)—The name of this mountain is a play on God's name, Jehovah-Jireh. Both names carry the meaning of the provision of the Lord, which will be "seen." Put another way, God will "see to it" and it will "be seen." (See also verse 14.)

For your information, Solomon would later build a great temple to God on this same mountain (2 Chronicles 3:1).

— *Distance* (verse 4)—Abraham and Isaac traveled 50-60 miles from Beersheba to Mount Moriah in three days. (Don't forget to look at the map on page 153.)

4. Now read Genesis 22:9-14. Once Abraham and Isaac arrived at the designated place, what did Abraham do (verse 9)?

What was his next move (verse 10)?

(Can you imagine?!) But, what is the first word of verse 11?

What was the message to Abraham (verse 12)?

And what message had Abraham's actions communicated to the Lord (verse 12)?

Describe what happened next (verse 13).

What name did Abraham give this special place and why (verse 14)?

...and Your Heart's Answer

In this passage of Scripture, Sarah's husband Abraham was literally walking with God step by step as he obeyed God's initial command, packed up the items (and Isaac!) for the sacrifice, and set out on a three-day journey to the place God had designated, walking step by step...for three whole days...right up to Mount Moriah.

• Up until this event, how had Abraham and Sarah demonstrated their faith in God according to these verses from Hebrews 11?

Verse 8–

Verses 9-10–

Verse 11–

What does Hebrews 11:17-19 have to say about the scene and the test of faith detailed in this lesson?

• And did Abraham ever pass the test!!! Hear these eloquent words:

> *No* test could have been more severe than the one God now imposed. And no obedience could have been more perfect than Abraham's....He [was called upon] to give evidence of absolute obedience and unquestioning trust in Jehovah...[to] obey blindly, proceeding step by step until [his] faith stood out as clearly as the noonday sun. Abraham passed through the fiercest fires, stood up under the mightiest pressure, and endured the most difficult strain, to emerge from the trial in complete tri- umph.[41]

As I thought about the drama and the scale of God's request to Abraham to offer up his only son, my mind, of course, flew to Romans 8:32. Note its message now.

• But what about you and me and the pattern of our walk in this area of obedience? What "sacrifices" of obedience are we offering up or could we offer up as a love offering to God? I think, as a woman, a wife, a mother, and a daughter, that the following verses reflect valid "steps" of obedience and tests of love. Note God's "commands":

As a woman—1 Timothy 5:10

As a wife—Titus 2:4

As a mother—Titus 2:4

As a daughter—Exodus 20:12 and Ephesians 6:2-3

Check any of these areas where your submission to God's Word is lagging. Then make plans, purpose in your heart, and pray for God's grace to obey His commands. For what did Jesus say in John 14:15?

From the Heart

Beloved, Abraham's faith shone, as the earlier quote described it, "as the noonday sun." Why? Because he believed in and acted upon God's promise. Someone has queried as follows:

> "In Isaac shall thy seed be called"–there was a
>   promise.
>
> "Offer Isaac for a burnt-offering"–there was a
>   command.
>
> How did Abraham reconcile them? He did not,
>   he could not.
>
> He simply obeyed the command, and God ful-
>   filled the promise.[42]

But now we must move from Abraham to you, dear one. Consider again this crowning scene from Abraham's life from Genesis 22 alongside the words of Jesus in Luke 14:26. Then ponder this question: Are you willing to sacrifice all?

Receiving God's Blessings

Genesis 22:15-24

o you remember our previous lesson? Do you remember Abraham raising his knife over his only son, Isaac?

I know I was holding my breath...until I read those wonderful words, "But the Angel of the LORD called to him from heaven and said, "Do not lay your hand on the lad, or do anything to him; for now I know that you fear God, since you have not withheld your son, your only son, from Me" (Genesis 22:11-12). As one has said, "Abraham withheld nothing, and God gave him everything."[43]

We'll look more into the blessings granted to Abraham in a minute. For now, though, let's see how this story ends, and how this chapter ends.

God's Input...

So far, Abraham was asked by God to offer his son Isaac as a burnt offering. We noted that Abraham's obedience was instant. He traveled to the prescribed place. He built an altar. He bound his son. He laid his son on the altar. He lifted his knife over his son.

However, God interrupted and halted the whole act. Abraham then spotted a ram caught by its horns in a thicket, which he offered in Isaac's place. It was an awesome experience (we can be sure!), and so Abraham named the place "The-LORD-Will-Provide." And that's where we join the Bible text today.

1. Read Genesis 22:15-19. *Who* called to Abraham again from heaven (verse 15)?

   What was His message to Abraham (verses 16-18)? Be sure to list each "promise."

   Compare this message of blessing with Genesis 13:16 and Genesis 15:5.

   How does this scene end (verse 19)?

2. Now read Genesis 22:20-24. This may not look very important, but the "blessings" have begun! God promised that He would make of Abraham a great nation. The news from afar was to be part of that blessing. What was the message (verse 20)?

Who was Milcah (see Genesis 11:29)?

And who was Nahor (see Genesis 11:27 and 29)?

Note especially Genesis 22:23. What was to become of Rebekah (see Genesis 24:67)?

...and Your Heart's Answer

- Abraham obeyed...and God blessed. Blessings can be ours, too, as we walk in obedience. So how's your obedience quotient? Make a few notes here of your answers and why you answered as you did.

Is God first in your life? Even before family members?

Are you a faithful and attentive wife, mother, daughter?

Do you carry your loved ones in your heart, praying earnestly for them?

Are there any known areas of disobedience in your life?

What are your plans for change in these areas of disobedience?

Are you held in high esteem by others because of your character?

Are you a blessing to others?

From the Heart

"The-LORD-Will-Provide." We now know that this is the name Abraham gave the place where God provided a ram to take the place of Isaac. But did you know that this is also a name for God? We mentioned in the previous lesson that *Jehovah-Jireh* means "The LORD will provide."

And, dear one, this is a powerful promise you and I can draw on at any time. Whenever you feel overwhelmed by something you've been asked to do or something that is expected of you, and you just can't see *how* you can do it, remember—and believe!—"The LORD will provide." God's role is to provide. Ours is to walk in obedience with complete trust in Him! Check out these scenarios:

> The Red Sea did not part until Moses lifted his hand and his rod (Exodus 14:16,21).

> The waters of the Jordan did not divide until the priests stepped into them (Joshua 3:13).

> Rahab's family wasn't saved until she tied a scarlet thread in her window (Joshua 2:21).

> The widow's oil didn't increase until she poured it out (2 Kings 4:5).

Naaman's leprosy wasn't cured until he washed in the Jordan River seven times (2 Kings 5:14)!

In every one of these situations, the blessing occurred only *after* faith acted—just like it did with Abraham. And in every case the predicament was impossible—just like it was for Abraham! And in every case God pressed His dear children right up to the edge...until common sense and reason had to be abandoned and faith was forced to bloom, until the "seen" had to be replaced with faith that is "unseen." This is exactly the way it was for Abraham. And, dear one, it's exactly the way it is for you.[44]

Now, name your greatest challenge. Then note the steps of obedience *and* faith that you must take to behold the gracious blessings of God. Remember, "The LORD will provide"!

Lesson 24

Saying Good-bye to Sarah
Genesis 23:1-20

*L*ess than a week ago, my husband and I attended the memorial service of our daughter Courtney's mother-in-law, Lois. Our experience at that ceremony certainly lived out the paradoxical couplets *glad/sad, bitter-sweet,* and *joyous sorrow.* Yes, we sat and grieved—selfishly for our loss, for the voids created in the lives of so many by the departure of a wife, a mother, a grandmother, a sister, and a friend. We sniffed and cried for the duration of the two-hour service.

Yet Lois's service was a celebration! The minister read assuring promises of eternal life from the Bible. Family and friends alike rose to their feet and honored Lois by sharing warm memories and kind words. We sang her favorite hymns. As the details of her 58 years of life were recounted, we were all amazed at God's goodness and God's grace, not only to Lois but to each of us as well. In our hearts we were glad for Lois, whose bout with cancer is now forever over and who is face-to-face with her Lord, in a place where she will never again suffer tears, death, sorrow, crying, or pain (Revelation 21:3-4)! Each of us left comforted and encouraged.

Well, beloved, today we are saddened to lay our dear Sarah to rest. All things must come to an end, and that's true of Sarah's life, too.

And God's account of Sarah's death and burial is unique in that her age at death is recorded in the Bible, the details of her burial and funeral are given in Scripture. Let's see what else God has for us to learn.

God's Input...

1. Read Genesis 23:1-2 and locate Hebron on your map. How old was Sarah when she died (verse 1)?

   Where did she die (verse 2)?

   And how did Abraham respond to her death (verse 2)?

2. Now read Genesis 23:3-15. First we have Abraham's appeal. To whom did he speak (verse 3)?

   And what was his request (verse 4)?

   How was his request received (verses 5-6)?

Which piece of land did Abraham specifically ask to buy (verses 7-9)?

And what was the response to his offer (verses 10-11)?

What was Abraham's final request (verses 12-13)?

How did this scene end (verses 14-15)?

For your information...death and burial involved many rituals and traditions. It was Abraham's responsibility to properly honor Sarah. Also what we are witnessing here is polite but typical bargaining that went something like this...

> Move #1   I need to buy a piece of land.

> Move #2   Of course. Choose the finest.

> Move #3   Please sell me this piece.

> Move #4   Oh no, you take it.

> Move #5   Oh no, let me buy it.

> Move #6   OK. You can buy it.

3. Finally, and to end our study, read Genesis 23:16-20. God is very specific in these verses about Abraham's property (which, by the way, is the only property he ever purchased!), but what is the key event here (verse 19)?

How is Abraham's newly purchased property described in verse 20?

Note who else was buried alongside Sarah:

Genesis 25:9-10–

Genesis 49:29-32–

Genesis 50:13–

And now for an inspiring word regarding the death of these saints:

> "These all died in faith" [says Hebrews 11:13]: the importance of this chapter lies in this. By leaving their bones in Canaan the patriarchs gave their last witness to the promise.... "While they themselves were silent...the sepulchre cried aloud, that death formed no obstacle to their entering on the possession of it."[45]

...and Your Heart's Answer

In our final lesson, we'll look back at the whole of Sarah's life. But for now here are a few practical lessons to take to heart from the life of Abraham.

• *Dealing with death*—What lessons does Abraham teach us about dealing with the death of a loved one?

- *Dealing with men*—Describe Abraham's manner in dealing with the men of Heth.

How is his character revealed through his treatment of these pagans?

How did these men view Abraham?

What lessons can you learn here about interpersonal relationships?

From the Heart

Our Sarah is gone! But she lives on, not only in our hearts, but also in God's inerrant, inspired, infallible, eternal Word. We can always enjoy a fresh visit with Sarah. She's always there—and always will be—just a page away, right in our Bible.

Surely a deep void was left in Abraham's life! We're not told how long they were married, but we can count at least 25 years of marriage up until Isaac's birth. We also know that Sarah died at 127, making it a good 62 (and probably more) years of marriage that we can account for!

Sarah was, as we say today, "the love of Abraham's life." Theirs had been a genuine and tender love, and Sarah was truly Abraham's "princess." *He* was a man of great faith. And *she* was a woman of great faith. We can only imagine the support each gave to the other's faith as they wandered about those many decades following the call of God.

May you and I, dear woman after God's own heart, be faithful to follow in the godly Sarah's footsteps. When we do, when we walk by faith, when we trust in God and His promises, then, as 1 Peter 3:6 promises, we become her "daughters."

Lesson 25

Looking at Life Lessons from Sarah

I was blessed to read the following prayer about the account of Sarah's life story written by Scottish theologian, devotional writer, and hymn composer George Matheson.

> *We* bless You for this portrait, O God. We are glad that at the opening of the Gallery You placed a picture of fair womanhood wearing no bonds. We are grateful for the primitive vision of a mistress of the home. May the world never outgrow this picture; may it be the guiding-star for all time! May the hearth of Sarah ever be brightened by her own hand!...

Let her make allowance for the clouds in the masculine sky! Let her believe that her first impression was the true one! Let her hold fast to the ideal of her youth! May her devotion be undimmed by the desert! May her care not corrode in the conflict!...Then shall her evening and her morning be one cloudless day![46]

What a lovely look at our Sarah, a princess and a mother of nations! Truly, as one character sketch on Sarah's life listed: "Occupation—wife, mother, and household manager"[47] Clearly this eloquent prayer and character sketch accurately portrays the heart and life of dear Sarah!

God's Input...

As we take a last look at lessons from Sarah's life, look again and make note of these scriptures:

Psalm 105:13-15–

Isaiah 51:2–

Romans 4:19; 9:9–

Hebrews 11:11–

1 Peter 3:6–

...and Your Heart's Answer

As I looked at Sarah's long life and sought to draw lessons from it, I made this acrostic.

S-ubmissive—left homeland and followed her husband as he followed God. This meant a nomadic lifestyle (Hebrews 11:9-10).

A-mazed—at the Angel of the LORD's announcement...and laughed.

R-ationalized—and gave Hagar to Abraham for a child.

A-ncestor of Jesus Christ.

H-opeful—for a child.

Now, you are welcome to try your hand at your own acrostic for S-A-R-A-H. But more importantly, I want you to use your own name and create an acrostic on page 152 that describes *you*! Please give this some thought. It's also a good idea to get input from husband and family and friends. This will be an invaluable exercise! I promise!

From the Heart

I'm always saddened by good-byes. And that's the emotion going on right this minute in my own heart as we're saying good-bye to Sarah and as I say good-bye to you, my dear sister and faithful traveling companion.

But before we do actually go our separate ways, I have a final question for you.

"Waiting" was one of the overarching themes in dear Sarah's life. And so I ask you, for what are *you* waiting?

Waiting is defined as "remaining inactive in readiness of expectation." For what are you remaining inactive in readiness of? Are you waiting for a prodigal to return to his or her Father? Or are you waiting for release from some physical affliction? Perhaps you are waiting for a husband—or for your husband to return to the Lord, or to love the Lord more deeply, or to be the spiritual leader in your home. Could it be you are waiting, like our Sarah, for a baby? Or are you waiting for vindication from some unfortunate misunderstanding, for God to come to your rescue and show forth His righteousness on your behalf (Psalm 37:6)? Are you eagerly waiting for heaven, for the groaning of your body to cease, for your ultimate victory, to go home to the heavenly abode for which you so long?

God bids you and me to wait—in readiness and expectation, and to walk—in God's promises—just as Sarah did, whose sister you are as you trust in God (1 Peter 3:5-6).[48]

An Acrostic of My Name

Abraham and Sarah's Travels

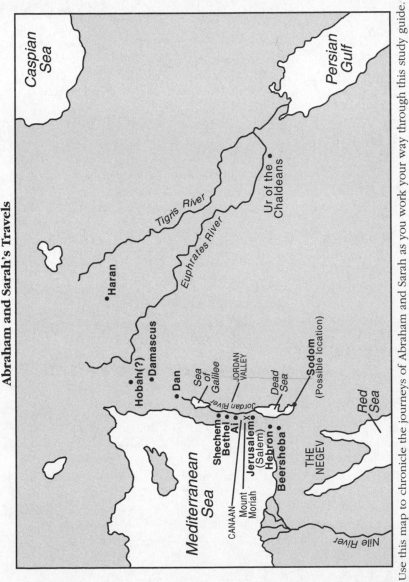

Use this map to chronicle the journeys of Abraham and Sarah as you work your way through this study guide.

Notes

1. Taken from Elizabeth George, *A Woman After God's Own Heart™* (Eugene, OR: Harvest House Publishers, 1997), pp. 24-29.

2. N. Avigad and Y. Yadin, *A Genesis Apocryphon* (Jerusalem: Magnes Press, 1956), cols. 20:6f.

3. From a Jewish commentary on Proverbs 31:10, *Midrash Michle* 31.

4. W. Gunther Plant, *The Torah: A Modern Commentary* (New York: Union of American Hebrew Congregations, 1981), p. 158.

5. Derek Kidner, *Genesis* (Downers Grove, IL: Intervarsity Press, 1973), p. 111.

6. Drawn from Neil S. Wilson, ed., *The Handbook of Bible Application* (Wheaton, IL: Tyndale House Publishers, Inc.,1992), pp. 501-02.

7. Gene A. Getz, *Abraham: Trials & Triumphs* (Glendale, CA: Regal Books Division, G/L Publications, 1976), p. 17.

8. William J. Petersen and Randy Peterson, *The One Year Book of Psalms* (Wheaton, IL: Tyndale House Publishers, Inc., 1999), March 25.

9. Matthew Henry, *Commentary on the Whole Bible—Volume 1* (Peabody, MA: Hendrickson Publishers, 1996), p. 70.

10. Civilla D. Martin, "His Eye Is on the Sparrow."

11. Getz, *Abraham: Trials & Triumphs,* pp. 34-38.

12. William J. Petersen and Randy Petersen, *The One Year Book of Psalms*, March 10.

13. Robert Jamieson, A. R. Fausset, and David Brown, *Commentary on the Whole Bible* (Grand Rapids, MI: Zondervan Publishing House, 1973), p. 26.

14. *Life Application Bible* (Wheaton, IL: Tyndale House Publishers, Inc., 1988), p. 25.

15. Ibid., p. 28.

16. Henry, *Commentary on the Whole Bible—Volume 1,* p. 78.

17. Getz, *Abraham: Trials & Triumphs,* p. 75.

18. *Life Application Bible,* p. 30.

19. Ben Patterson, *Waiting—Finding Hope When God Seems Silent* (Downers Grove, IL: InterVarsity Press, 1989), p. 10.

20. Jamieson, Fausset, and Brown, *Commentary on the Whole Bible,* p. 27.

21. Kidner, *Genesis,* pp. 128-29.

22. Ibid., p. 130.

23. G. Campbell Morgan, *Life Applications from Every Chapter of the Bible* (Grand Rapids, MI: Fleming H. Revell, 1994), p. 12.

24. John H. Sammis, "Trust and Obey."

25. Elizabeth George, *Women Who Loved God—365 Days with the Women of the Bible* (Eugene, OR: Harvest House Publishers, 1999), January 21.

26. William T. Summers, ed., *3000 Quotations from the Writings of Matthew Henry* (Grand Rapids, MI: Fleming H. Revell, 1982), p. 149.

27. Roy B. Zuck, ed., *The Speaker's Quote Book,* quoting H. G. Salter (Grand Rapids, MI: Kregel Publications, 1997), p. 320.

28. Charles F. Pfeiffer and Everett F. Harrison, eds., *The Wycliffe Bible Commentary* (Chicago: Moody Press, 1972), p. 25.

29. Getz, *Abraham: Trials & Triumphs,* p. 57.

30. John MacArthur, *The MacArthur Study Bible* (Nashville, TN: Word Publishing, 1997), p. 41.

31. Getz, *Abraham: Trials & Triumphs,* p. 57.

32. Ibid.

33. Pfeiffer and Harrison, eds., *The Wycliffe Bible Commentary,* p. 26.

34. Kidner, *Genesis,* p. 138.

35. Ibid., p. 139.

36. Author unknown.

37. George, *Women Who Loved God—365 Days with the Women of the Bible,* January 29.

38. Ibid., February 2.

39. Pfeiffer and Harrison, eds., *The Wycliffe Bible Commentary,* p. 27.

40. George, *Women Who Loved God—365 Days with the Women of the Bible,* January 29.

41. Pfeiffer and Harrison, eds., *The Wycliffe Bible Commentary*, p. 27.

42. D. L. Moody, *Notes from My Bible & Thoughts from My Library*, quoting Hector Hall (Grand Rapids, MI: Baker Book House, 1979), p. 15.

43. Moody, *Notes from My Bible & Thoughts from My Library*, p. 22.

44. Drawn from Elizabeth George, *The Lord Is My Shepherd* (Eugene, OR: Harvest House Publishers, 2000), pp. 38-40.

45. Kidner, *Genesis*, quoting John Calvin, p. 145.

46. George Matheson, *Portraits of Bible Women* (Grand Rapids, MI: Kregel Publications, 1993), pp. 42-43.

47. *Life Application Bible,* p. 35.

48. Drawn from George, *Women Who Loved God—365 Days with the Women of the Bible,* January 28.

About the Author

Elizabeth George is a bestselling author whose passion is to teach the Bible in a way that changes women's lives. She has more than 7 million books in print, including *A Woman After God's Own Heart*® and *A Woman's Daily Walk with God*.

For information about Elizabeth, her books, and her ministry, and to sign up to receive her daily devotions, and to join her on Facebook and Twitter, visit her website at:

www.ElizabethGeorge.com

BIBLE STUDIES *for*

BUSY WOMEN

Character Studies

Old Testament Studies

New Testament Studies

Books by Elizabeth George

- Beautiful in God's Eyes
- Breaking the Worry Habit...Forever
- Finding God's Path Through Your Trials
- Following God with All Your Heart
- The Heart of a Woman Who Prays
- Life Management for Busy Women
- Loving God with All Your Mind
- Loving God with All Your Mind DVD and Workbook
- A Mom After God's Own Heart
- A Mom After God's Own Heart Devotional
- Moments of Grace for a Woman's Heart
- One-Minute Inspiration for Women
- Quiet Confidence for a Woman's Heart
- Raising a Daughter After God's Own Heart
- The Remarkable Women of the Bible
- Small Changes for a Better Life
- Walking With the Women of the Bible
- A Wife After God's Own Heart
- A Woman After God's Own Heart®
- A Woman After God's Own Heart® Deluxe Edition
- A Woman After God's Own Heart®— Daily Devotional
- A Woman's Daily Walk with God
- A Woman's Guide to Making Right Choices
- A Woman's High Calling
- A Woman's Walk with God
- A Woman Who Reflects the Heart of Jesus
- A Young Woman After God's Own Heart
- A Young Woman After God's Own Heart— A Devotional
- A Young Woman's Guide to Prayer
- A Young Woman's Guide to Making Right Choices

Study Guides

- Beautiful in God's Eyes Growth & Study Guide
- Finding God's Path Through Your Trials Growth & Study Guide
- Following God with All Your Heart Growth & Study Guide
- Life Management for Busy Women Growth & Study Guide
- Loving God with All Your Mind Growth & Study Guide
- Loving God with All Your Mind Interactive Workbook
- A Mom After God's Own Heart Growth & Study Guide
- The Remarkable Women of the Bible Growth & Study Guide
- Small Changes for a Better Life Growth & Study Guide
- A Wife After God's Own Heart Growth & Study Guide
- A Woman After God's Own Heart® Growth & Study Guide
- A Woman's Call to Prayer Growth & Study Guide
- A Woman's High Calling Growth & Study Guide
- A Woman Who Reflects the Heart of Jesus Growth & Study Guide

Children's Books

- A Girl After God's Own Heart
- A Girl After God's Own Heart Devotional
- God's Wisdom for Little Girls
- A Little Girl After God's Own Heart

Books by Jim George

- 10 Minutes to Knowing the Men and Women of the Bible
- The Bare Bones Bible® Handbook
- The Bare Bones Bible® for Teens
- A Boy After God's Own Heart
- A Husband After God's Own Heart
- Know Your Bible from A to Z
- A Leader After God's Own Heart
- A Man After God's Own Heart
- A Man After God's Own Heart Devotional
- The Man Who Makes a Difference
- One-Minute Insights for Men
- A Young Man After God's Own Heart
- A Young Man's Guide to Making Right Choices

Books by Jim & Elizabeth George

- A Couple After God's Own Heart
- A Couple After God's Own Heart Interactive Workbook
- God's Wisdom for Little Boys
- A Little Boy After God's Own Heart